T0128732

While I Was Musing, the Fire Burned

Michael P. Petrillo, PhD

iUniverse, Inc.
Bloomington

While I Was Musing, the Fire Burned

iUniverse books may be ordered through booksellers or by contacting:

iUniverse
1663 Liberty Drive
Bloomington, IN 47403
www.iuniverse.com
1-800-Authors (1-800-288-4677)

ISBN: 978-1-4620-6296-6 (sc)
ISBN: 978-1-4620-6297-3 (hc)
ISBN: 978-1-4620-6298-0 (ebook)

Library of Congress Control Number: 2011919554

Printed in the United States of America

iUniverse rev. date: 11/04/2011

SEVEN KEYS TO SPIRITUAL ENLIGHTENMENT

I.   Symbols

II.   Sayings and Quotations

III.   Synergism and Synchronism

IV.   Spiritual Wisdom and Inner Light

V.   Sage: The Wonderful, Wise, Wizard Within

VI.   Serenity

VII.   Synthesis

WISDOM said—

"Open thy heart to me and I shall fill it with light."

Voice of the Master, Khalil Gibran

CONTENTS

Part I Beginnings

Introduction   **3**
One   My Story   5
Two   Family, Discovery, and Early Mentors   13
Three   Friendships and Symbols   17
Four   Mentors, Christianity, and Change   22
Five   Loss and New Direction   28
Six   Spiritual Journeys   32
Seven   Seeking with an Open Mind   44
Eight   Change and New Goals   49
Nine   Starting Over   58
Ten   A Mystic Soul Evokes The Muse   71

Part II The Seven Keys to Spiritual Enlightenment

Eleven   Key I Symbols, Dreams, and Interpretations   87
Twelve   Key II Sayings, Quotations, and Meditation   98
Thirteen   Key III Synergism, Synchronism, and Poetry   118
Fourteen   Key IV Spiritual Wisdom and Inner Light   127
Fifteen   Key V Wise Wizard Within   137
Sixteen   Key VI Evoking Serenity   149
Seventeen   Key VII Synthesis, Intuition, and Musing   163

PART I

BEGINNINGS

INTRODUCTION

I love stories, true or not. I have always collected them. The following stories are woven together telling of my life and the people who participated in it and influenced me. Other people, of course, told some of the first stories I remember. How I reacted is neither good nor bad. I simply reacted from what I was able to understand at the time and from what I made of the stories. Reactions and interpretations are personal and are not to be taken literally. They simply are like seeds planted in a fertile mind that take root and produce fruit for mental digestion and enlightenment.

The Peekskill of my youth was a village on the Hudson River in New York. The area surrounding Peekskill was made up of other small villages and many lakes, making water an important stimulus in my life.

As a child, I enjoyed a great deal of freedom with my extended family of older brothers, uncles, and cousins. Together we fished, we swam, we went boating, and we listened to the tales of riverfront towns along the Hudson River.

When I grew much older, I was surprised to read a H.U.D. report that summed up the area where I grew up. Peekskill suffered the most extreme poverty, the worst housing, and the highest crime rate in the state of New York. Oblivious to those facts in my younger years, I thrived and enjoyed life.

Chapter 1

My Story

During a cold January blizzard in Peekskill at 4 in the morning, my mother Esther Mae went into labor. Since we did not own a car, my father Tony called Mom's cousins who owned the local taxi service. They came immediately and took Mom to the Peekskill Community Hospital where Dr. Sweet, our family doctor, was waiting. So at 4:30 am on January 7, 1927, I was born. I weighed over 12 pounds.

I was the second son of Tony and Esther. Brother Fred was fifteen years my senior. Fred described me as a child by saying that I went from crawling to running in a very short time, filled with energy and enthusiasm and always eager to learn. Mom laughed at that and said that I skipped learning to walk.

When my brother Vincent was born on December 9, 1931, two big changes took place in my life besides having a new little brother. For one, Dad realized our apartment was too small for the growing family. He found us a new place to live on upper Division Street in Peekskill where we had more room. I was four years eight months old and still running all the time. It took a great deal of Mom's time to keep me busy, which led Mom to make the second change.

Mom decided to enroll me in kindergarten shortly before Vincent's birth. That gave Mom an opportunity to spend more time with Vincent, and it gave me an outlet for my energy. I started school at Oak Street Grammar School as the youngest student enrolled.

Big brother Fred took me to school each day since Dad was working from 4 am till 9 or 10 pm seven days a week. We took our hard lives for granted then since we knew little else. Not seeing Dad very often meant that my brother Fred became a dad to me, which is a story to be told!

Fred was a husky, strong youth. He quit school at 16 to work with Uncle Tom at the New York Central Railroad repairing track up and down the Hudson River shoreline.

Fred left for work about 5 am each day, came home to take me to school about 7:30, and then returned to work. When his hours permitted, he also brought me home from school. Fred played an important role in my life. He was Mom's favorite, my surrogate dad, and my buddy and teacher about life both good and bad.

Although Dad was raised as a Roman Catholic, he no longer attended church. He did, however, have all five of his sons baptized as Roman Catholics. Mom, an Episcopalian, went to Eucharistic Services in the morning and worked at the Salvation Army in the evenings. She became a soldier and was dedicated to the Army and all its good deeds for the poor. I went to the Episcopal Church on Sunday mornings and the Salvation Army in the evenings. I loved both but had more fun and enjoyed the music and singing at the Salvation Army Headquarters. My aunt and my cousins were all Salvationists as well. My psyche was already ecumenical! I went from mass to merry music and singing. Mom sang solos and had a lovely voice. Dad, however, would have nothing to do with either! He continued to work hard seven days a week, and we continued to be very poor.

In spite of my early training, I was not really religious. I did not go to church school nor participate in church classes. I simply attended occasionally. Mom said I often slept during Mass and loved to sing and rattle the tambourine in the evenings during the Salvation Army Service.

Fred was now working full time for the New York Central Railroad. He continued to drop me off at school early before the school opened, and at times it was bitterly cold. The janitor was a kind man who let me stay in the furnace room to keep warm until school opened.

My first teacher was Miss Durkey, one of the most caring and warm people I ever knew. Soon a problem arose for me in Miss Durkey's class, however. I spoke like a street kid, which is what I was!

Miss Durkey visited our home to talk to my parents about my speech. Then she discovered that Dad still spoke Italian street-talk at home. Miss Durkey then knew the source of the problem. She told my dad to speak English only and that it was time to drop the street talk. Mom and I worried about the reaction Dad would have. Mom told me later that he was so shocked that he said nothing but just complied!

Soon after that we moved again, this time to The Flats. Today we would call them slums, but my dad was still not able to afford much more. The rent was $20 a month, and that was difficult for us. It was a grim place to live and we were eager to move on. We finally found an apartment on Main Street above a barbershop and my uncle's shoe repair shop. It was a much happier place to live. And I was getting older and it gave me a whole new area to explore and new friends to meet.

Shortly after our move to Main Street, I discovered a special weekend Halloween event at the Peekskill Theater. I decided it would be great fun to sneak in and enjoy the films. It took place all day lasting till nearly 12 midnight. There were hours of horror films to sit and squirm through and thoroughly enjoy! The last film was the classic Frankenstein! It was great fun for a young boy.

The film ended late, and I started home with a group of friends. My friends lived closer to the theater than I did. Each one left the group as he reached home, and I soon found myself alone in the dark. I hurried past the stores, which were closed. Suddenly, a man came out of a dark doorway and tried to grab me. I ran as fast as I could as the man chased me for half a mile uphill on Main Street, cursing and yelling for me to stop. At the top of Main Street, I saw the home of a good friend. The house was dark, but I ran between the hedges and under the porch where my friend and I often played hide and seek. I crawled around to the back of the house where I curled up under the back porch steps. I had hidden under the steps playing hide and seek many times before.

The man was thrashing around in the bushes yelling for me to show myself. Suddenly, all the lights on the back and front porches came on. The boy's father came out and shouted to the man to get out of the yard or get shot! Then I knew I would soon be safe!

I was still shaking with fear and anger though, so I stayed under the stairs till all the lights went out and everything was quiet again. Then I crawled out and hurried through their back yard to the street and ran the rest of the way home.

It was very late when I reached home, sneaked up the stairs to the bathroom, washed my hands and face with cold water, and crawled into bed. Mom heard me and came into my room.

"What's wrong?" she asked.

Still shaking, I blurted out where I had been that day and what had happened on the way home. I worried I would be in trouble again! But Mom hugged me and reassured me. She said, "You did good!"

Mom knew that I didn't need to be told how much danger I had been in. But I knew I must be ever more watchful. My body now knew a fear of someone coming up behind me and surprising me. It took some growing for me to learn to get those fears under control.

That part of me remained behind the scenes and out of sight for years. However, when I was attacked, bloodied, hurt, or frightened, the hidden part jumped out and the fury was unleashed. I called him my sleeping grizzly!

When I was about 9 years old, an Italian bully named John punched me in the face, bloodied my nose, pounded my chest, and hit me below the belt. I backed away till I reached a chain-link fence on the playground. Finally, the angry sleeping grizzly came out. I fought back, beating him with hammer blows till I was pulled off. It made me shake with inner terror that he could bring out such rage in me. I didn't understand at the time where the rage came from. I now know it was a reflection of the terror I had felt when Pop got drunk and beat me. Mom always intervened before Pop would stop, but that terror of his anger never left me.

A similar event happened at college. One of my many jobs was to work with a partner checking the outside doors on campus at midnight to be certain that they were locked. One night I was hurrying since it was late and I still had studying to do. I tested one of the doors and turned to go to the next building. I was passing a bush when my partner jumped out trying to scare me. He thought it was funny. I was startled, and without thinking I turned around and hit him under the chin so hard that it lifted him off the ground and nearly knocked him out. We were both finally able to laugh about the event, but it did take some time to reach that point.

Many years later when I was at the church in Livermore, I went down the hallway to turn off all the lights at the end of the day on my way out the front entrance. I didn't know that one of our women members was still working in a classroom. She came out behind me and playfully tapped my back. I instantly turned around and without thinking lifted her off the hallway floor at least two feet. It was totally shocking for both of us that I would react so strongly. She was frightened, but she finally cried out to me.

"Oh, I'm sorry. I didn't mean to scare you!" I put her down and we looked at each other laughing.

Going home from the Livermore church that night, I realized that my response was a reaction to that old fear. The fear was still there, though it did not come out very often. I knew it was time to face my fears.

I dealt with my fear responses in therapy. I relayed how I was still hyper-reactive to any threat of someone coming up behind me. I learned the potential hazards of practical jokes, and I knew that I didn't want to repeat my fear reaction ever again. This led me to realize that we all have a little savage within that could become violent if our lives were threatened. The challenge was to learn to control the fear reactions. With thought and meditation over a period of years, I have learned to overcome the fears.

Chapter 2

FAMILY, DISCOVERY, AND
EARLY MENTORS

In Peekskill, winter was wonderful, white, cold and fun for all of us. One snowy day while sliding down a hill on a sled when I was about 7, a kid suddenly cut me off by bumping against my sled. I ricocheted out of control and sailed under a road barrier out into traffic. A car hit my sled, crushing it, while I hit the oil pan under the car, suffering a wound to my forehead and the loss of several teeth. When I came to, I was screaming, vomiting, and barely conscious, but I remember that my brother Fred appeared and took me to the hospital. That event affected me deeply, and today I cannot crawl into tight places without anxiety and some nausea. However, the accident did lead to a wonderful self-discovery soon after.

I was home recuperating for some time. In the long hours while I waited to heal, I developed a love for daydreaming and reading. These were two new discoveries for me that became increasingly important over the years. I would later realize that I was becoming a Muse.

I loved my mother completely. She was fun to be with, a great cook, and a wonderful nurturer. She was also a spiritual, earthy woman who loved her family.

Her green eyes were as changeable as the ocean and an indicator of her many moods. When she was impish and playful with her bubbling laugh, her eyes were clear, bright, and alive. When she went into her psychic self, reading tea leaves, acting as mid-wife, or counseling her large number of women friends, her eyes were grey, distant, and mysterious.

Mom had a flashing temper. When she was angry, her eyes changed from clear sea green to grey, stormy, and dangerous. I got out of the way when I saw that look in her eyes and dared not cross her.

When I was sick or had a wound, Mom became the Medicine Woman in the tribe. Our pantry was her medicine chest with herbs and mixtures of medicinal weeds for healing, plus the traditional cold alcohol baths for fevers, and ex-lax for elimination. She had a remedy for everything for those who came to her for help.

One day when Mom and I were uptown, a small boy came out of a nearby shop and began choking. He was beginning to turn blue when his mother came out. She began screaming. Mom rushed to the boy, lifted him by the heels, and slapped his back with one big swat! Out of his throat popped a marble. The boy was sobbing when Mom put him down and hugged him. His mother came up to hug him then, as Mom and I quietly walked away without saying a word. I was awed, but Mom was calm and went on without skipping a beat.

It took a lot to get Mom flustered. She was unflinchingly cool regardless of what was happening around her. With four sons and a hard working though hard-drinking husband, I think she had to be!

Mom sang much of the time. Music brought her happiness and peace. I can still tune in on her lullaby voice and the gospel songs she knew so well from her Salvation Army work as well as from being a member of the Episcopal Church. My mom was a healer to all who knew her, and one of my earliest mentors.

I loved to run, play marbles, swim, fish, climb, read, and sing when I was alone. I became very independent at a young age. When I was about seven, I hiked to a lake and climbed around on the cliffs above looking down into the water. I reached up to grab a rock above me, but the rock was loose and dropped down to the water. I fell 20 feet to the ice-covered glacial lake below, breaking the ice and sinking down to the bottom. Looking up, I remember watching bubbles and thinking that I would soon be dead. Suddenly, the cold shocked me awake! I became alert and was able to see light shining above the surface of the water, giving me a direction to swim to be safe. I climbed through the hole in the ice and hurried home. Mom made me strip off my clothes, spanked me, and cried all at the same time. Then she dried me off and put me to bed. I knew then that she loved me for sure. Her strength and love were a great influence in my life.

Chapter 3
FRIENDSHIPS AND SYMBOLS

It seemed to me that we were always moving. About the time I made friends in a neighborhood, we moved to another part of town. I now know that Dad was always looking for a better place for us to live. At the time, I just felt frustrated.

When I was 10, we moved again, this time to Main Street above an appliance and electronics store. While I lived there, I attended Oak Street Grammar School during 5th and 6th grades. One teacher, Miss Depew, deeply affected my life. She greatly encouraged my growing love of studying and reading books. Books were like friends to me that were always with me wherever I moved. Books always kept me company.

Since we moved often, we attended various churches. Since I had a variety of friends in each area of town where I lived, I often attended churches with them. I sat through many a Sunday service in Presbyterian, Lutheran, Methodist, Roman Catholic, and Independent churches. It was a wonderful introduction to many religions and helped to make me curious about their similarities and differences.

When I was about 13, my cousins and I attended a citywide youth rally at the Dutch Reform Church. The evangelist was a storyteller who kept my attention. I vividly remember his sermon.

Near the end, he read from Revelations 3:20.

"Behold! I stand at the door, and knock; if any man hear my voice and open the door, I will come in to him, and will sup with him, and he with me."

The evangelist symbolically told a story of Jesus standing at the door of our hearts. He knocked because there was no knob on the outside. We must open the door to let Him enter. I began to visualize the image until it became a mystical experience. I now know that I was musing. I could see my inner self listening to the voice of Jesus and hearing Him speak to me asking,

May I come in and be with you now and all of your life, teaching you to love God and yourself?

I saw myself reaching for the knob on the inside. I opened the door and invited Jesus to come into my heart. My whole body seemed filled with light, as He sat down with me and He communed His love, grace, and power.

I was very deeply moved by this experience. It stayed with me and guided my decisions about my future. Since the

Baptist Church sponsored the rally, I started to attend Sunday school at the First Baptist Church.

By junior high I had lived in one area long enough to have a number of friends to hang out with and do some of the wild things that teenagers do. An event happened then that shocked me deeply. M. R., one of my friends, and I were playing tag on top of the walls around the school. The walls were topped with chain link fencing. M. R. was standing outside the fence, and our friend Nick was trying to tag M. R.'s hands through the fence. M. R. pulled his hands back, lost his balance, and fell 8 to 10 feet to the ground. I jumped down and saw that he was knocked out with his legs at a weird angle. Since I was a boy scout, I had taken first aid and had training in splints. Several other kids wanted to move M. R., but I pushed them back. I called to Nick to find the janitor and tell him to call an ambulance. When the janitor came with a blanket, he took one look at M. R. and told me that I had done the right thing by not moving him. He warned that M.R.'s back could be broken, and if we tried to move him, it could sever his spine. Soon the ambulance arrived. Nick and I watched silently as it drove M. R. to the hospital.

The following day was Saturday, and I walked to my favorite spot in the Oak Park Woods where I had built a tree hut. I was deeply depressed and worried about my friend. I didn't know then how to label what I was doing, but I laid back and stared at the clouds moving slowly across the sky. I now know that I was again musing. As I became very peaceful, a thought came to my mind.

You did OK. Now go to Nick and tell him that he was not the cause of M. R.'s accident. Tell him we were all playing and having fun, but M. R. made a wrong move and fell. I would tell him that I was there, and I knew that Nick didn't push M.R.

I went to Nick's house and sat on the porch with him. I told him what I saw and that it wasn't his fault that M. R. had fallen. I suggested to Nick, "Let's go see M. R. when he comes home and take him some popcorn from your dad's store."

Nick agreed that it would be a good idea. When M. R. finally did get home, he was healing but still needed time to recover. He was very glad to see us.

M.R. said, "It's OK, Nick. You weren't at fault. I lost my balance and fell. Don't blame yourself."

Nick told me afterward how much I had helped him recover from feeling depressed and guilty. Nick was older than I was, but we remained friends for a number of years. Near the beginning of WWII, however, Nick was drafted and never returned.

One morning not long after that I remember walking to school alone and singing songs that I knew as I walked.

The verse from Revelations 3:20 popped into my head. "Here I am! I stand at the door and knock. If anyone hears my voice and opens the door, I will come in and eat with that person, and they with me." Again, I saw in my imagination a light. I saw the door. I remember Christ coming in to be with me. I asked what I should do now with my life. The answer popped into my mind. "I am with you; what do you want?" No one had ever asked me what I really wanted. I had no answer so I replied, "I don't know." The next sentence floored me. "Follow the light. I am the light of the world. Be peaceful and know that I am with you."

I then had my answer. My decision was made. "I want to follow you. Please light the way."

The answer was, "I am with you always, whatever you do or wherever you go."

It now seemed so simple. Seek more knowledge and do what I love. That made sense to me. I decided to enjoy school, love learning, go to church, and be with Christians.

Chapter 4

MENTORS, CHRISTIANITY, AND CHANGE

Soon after my decision, I listened to Les Chontos speak in our school auditorium. He was the Westchester County heavyweight champion weight lifter He talked to young men about healthy eating, a good physical body, and sex. Les didn't mince words. I liked what he said. Neither my mother nor father had ever talked to me about sex.

At the close of the meeting, I talked to Les about whether he was also a Christian. He replied, "Yes, and I'm inviting you to come to the First Baptist Church youth group as well as participate in all the groups in your school so you will have a life of broad experiences."

So I did! I got involved in chorus and sports, and decided to take my education seriously. Even though I was 14 and only a sophomore at Peekskill High, I decided to join every singing group I could, as well as drama clubs, verse choir, and the men's quartet. Singing opened many doors for me as it enabled me to give back a little bit in gratitude for my life.

Les had come into my life at the right moment. He became my mentor, friend, and teacher. He invited me to join him in a weight-lifting class at the local fire station called The Truck. I was no longer lost. I now had direction. I found that learning was enjoyable, not a chore!

By the time I was 16 and a junior in high school I was a good, though average, student. I enjoyed all that I was involved in including track and the swimming team. Part of my high school schedule was to work at the Mohegan Market in occupational training as a meat cutter. My life was busy, and I liked it that way.

During that year, I was still attending Sunday school at the First Baptist Church of Peekskill, New York. It was there that I met Buddy. Peggy, our teacher, was Buddy's aunt. Mary, Buddy's sister, and I also became friends.

Buddy and I led two lives. We were good Christians at church, attended youth groups, and worked as ushers. I was a tenor in the choir. The rest of the time, however, we were adventurous and mischievous. We roller skated with the youth group, partied, swam, boated, and of course, laughed a lot! Buddy was handsome and thought of himself as a lover. He always had more than one girlfriend at a time. I was more reserved, however, and usually focused on only one girl at a time.

At night, when Buddy's dad Ike was asleep, we would roll Ike's car out of the driveway in neutral and coast down the street before we started the motor. We always checked the gas gauge when we left and refilled it to the same level before we returned hours later. We had great fun cruising with friends, impressing the girls, going to movies, and just messing around being kids.

Buddy found a job as an usher at the Paramount Theater. He met a new group of friends at the theater, and soon began taking the train to New York City to meet them. He didn't tell me much, except to say that they would have parties and do stuff he didn't want to talk about. I admit that I felt bad about being left out.

On Tuesday morning, July 14, 1942, Buddy came into the Mohegan Market and asked me to join him on a trip to the city for a party. I was tempted and thought about it for some time, but my boss Mr. Clark told me that I couldn't have the time off. Buddy and I would have been gone from Tuesday till Wednesday evening, returning home by sneaking a ride on the train. I was disappointed that I couldn't go, but Buddy and I parted friends. His last words to me that day were brief.

"I'll see ya!"

Wednesday morning I was working at the market when Pastor Ham came in the store looking shaken and pale. He took me aside and, as compassionately as he could, told me that he had just been notified that a train had killed Buddy.

I was numb. Time stopped. I just stood staring ahead in shock. Then Pastor Ham told me that he couldn't face Ike alone to tell him what happened to his son.

"Will you come with me, Michael?"

Mr. Clark put his hand on my shoulder and told me to go, but also to take care of myself.

I got my jacket and Pastor Ham and I went to Buddy Yocum's home. Ike had received the news at work and had immediately come home. Since Ike knew me and what a friend I had been to Buddy, he sank into my arms sobbing. His wife and daughter joined us. We all stood hugging and crying. Pastor Ham enclosed us in his arms and prayed.

"There are no human words that are adequate to comfort such a loss. May I pray for comfort and the presence of Christ to envelop us?"

I don't remember much more about the day I lost my best friend. I know that I comforted others, but I was still in deep shock myself. I didn't cry. Pastor and I stayed with the Yocum family for a long time.

There were more notices from the police and the New York Central Rail Road, but although it was called an accident, the suspicion was planted in our minds that there might have been foul play. The police were vague. Nothing came of their suspicions.

Since the service for Buddy was set for Sunday, Saturday was for viewing of the body at the Yocum's home. I was the first one to come to view Buddy in the casket. His head had been crushed and cut off. The funeral director created a wax face and head with Buddy's hair on top. I was shocked. It looked so strange that I had to turn away. I ran home from the Yocums and locked myself in my room. I still could not cry, but for the first time, I knew I had to go inside of me to find an answer since the whole thing made no sense to me. I really didn't know anything about prayer except to repeat the Lord's Prayer at church. It was my first experience with the death of someone I loved as a brother, friend, and Buddy!

My mother Esther was a very spiritual person. She knew what I was experiencing. She knocked on my door and I immediately let her in my room. She asked that I go into complete silence and seek a message from within my spirit. She sat quietly with me for a long time. As she left my room she repeated that I be alone to meditate, even though I didn't know the full meaning of the word. "Sit in silence and something will come." I complied and turned my reading lamp on to light the corner of my room. Mom had kept my three brothers downstairs so I could be alone.

I was aware that Buddy's spirit wasn't in the casket. I remembered quite suddenly his last words to me. "I'll see ya." Then I began to cry, crying until I was totally exhausted. I finally fell into a deep sleep on my small bed.

I awoke feeling somewhat withdrawn as I came downstairs to the dining room for dinner. No one had spoken of Buddy or about his death that evening.

Later I made a call to a friend of Buddy's and mine. I asked him what had happened. He told me that he couldn't say because he would be in big trouble, but whispered, "I'll talk to you next week. Bye!"

It was the last time I spoke to him as his father suddenly sent him out of town. I never learned what really happened to Buddy.

I had to force myself to go to church that Sunday. It was a very somber occasion with lots of tears flowing. I hadn't felt comfortable since Buddy's death, and apparently, I was still in shock. I know now that it was an incubation period. Thinking about my own future, I realized that I wanted my own life to have purpose and meaning.

Chapter 5

LOSS AND NEW DIRECTION

After Buddy's death, I changed. I began to think things through more carefully before I made decisions. I would search both sides of issues and let it all simmer in the back of my mind. There were moments when I realized that I was having a shift in my energy and personality. I began reminding myself that any critical moment was an opportunity to relax, reflect, and wait for all the pieces to fall together before taking action. I was becoming a muse!

Becoming a muse meant weighing all the variables I could think of, releasing all consideration to my inner mind, and cogitating. I then sought illumination before making decisions.

By January 1944, the year of my 17th birthday, the war was being fought on several fronts. Patriotism was strong during those years. After a great deal of thought, I decided to join the United States Navy. Since I would graduate from Peekskill High School that year, I completed several tests and qualified for the Navy's V6 program that trained men to carry out technical tasks.

During that year I was hired by Skolsky's store, an upscale business in Peekskill that dealt in chinaware, jewelry, and toys. Les Chontos's wife Helen was also working at the store. Les had taken me under his wing, teaching me weightlifting, stamina training, and how to eat a healthy diet. I joined the Red Cross. I became one of the first teens to be a certified lifeguard. I also joined the Truck, a volunteer fireman's group, and soon was given the title of air raid warden. I patrolled the streets after dark, maintaining the Navy's ordered blackout rules. Many people feared that German submarines would perhaps invade the Hudson River towns.

I made a promise to Peg Yocum, my librarian friend, to read one book per week in addition to the National Geographic and the Student Edition of Time magazine. I also traveled with men's high school choir and performed at civic events including various service clubs like the Rotary. I became even more active at church and youth groups, which were led by Les. I also decided to stop dressing casually, and I began wearing suits, sport coats, and ties.

One Sunday the Bob Jones College Quartet visited our church. Their talent and enthusiasm impressed me. They were excellent singers. After the service, I met with Ernie Campbell, a tall, red-haired man and a student at Bob Jones College. Ernie had a winning personality. I told him that I had seriously thought of going on to college, but that I did not have enough money. He told me that he had a registration form and said, "Fill it in. I have a budget to pay for the costs."

Wow! I was sure the good Lord had tapped me on the head and said, "Do it!" So, I did!

Within three weeks I had received two letters. The first was a notice from the Navy to come to New York City to be sworn into the Navy's V6 program. The second letter was one of acceptance for me to become a student at Bob Jones College. It was time to make a choice.

I bought a train ticket to New York to the Navy's swearing-in ceremony and carried both letters with me to the event. I arrived at the center and there were over 200 kids my age in attendance. I sat in the back row and listened to the recruiter's speech with extreme interest. At the end, he stated, "Remember that when you swear your allegiance and take this oath, you are no longer a civilian. You are now in the Navy and we will determine your future. You are swearing to obey orders no matter what!"

That was when I got up from my seat and walked out to the desk where another recruiter was located. I showed him my letter from BJC and asked if he would please help me decide what to do regarding my future.

The recruiter looked at me and said, "Michael, if I were 17 and had a chance to attend college, I would go for two years. In two years you will be older and better able to make a decision as to what you want to do. The war will probably still be going on, but you will be a much better candidate to serve our country." He took my orders, tore them up, and crossed my name off the list. "Go for it, Michael!"

It sounded like God's voice giving me direction. On the way home, I decided that I would become a minister.

Chapter 6
SPIRITUAL JOURNEYS

The yearbook staff for 1944 grads was gathering material for the yearbook for the graduating class. My comment was that "Michael has decided to become a minister." The students who knew me during the "Buddy" days commented to me, "You have to be kidding!" I wasn't!

The church responded to my goals by setting up a fund for me. Ernie Campbell from Bob Jones College enrolled me in a work program to be one of the college meat cutters. It would pay enough for room and board, tuition, books, and other miscellaneous necessary expenses. In September of that year, I went to Cleveland, Tennessee, and began my spiritual journey, not knowing for sure where it would lead.

We all remember the events of 1945. The United States dropped two atomic bombs on Japan. That ended the war. That fall, I would be a junior in college.

While meditating, I was never sure of what would happen next, but it all seemed clear to me to follow my inner voice. I had learned to let go and listen carefully to what I was hearing. I had learned to let the still inner voice speak!

I headed into the unknown at age 17 to a small country town in Cleveland, Tennessee. Dr. Bob Jones, a well-known evangelist, founded Bob Jones College. I was pleasantly surprised at the curriculum and high quality of the drama and music programs. Since I was on a work-scholarship program and could not afford to live in a campus dorm, I was given a room in a residence that was converted to a house for about 8 to 10 students. In 2 years I earned enough money in the summer time to afford a room in the dorm with three roommates. Mostly the students were Southerners, so I was the token Northerner. I worked as a meat cutter at night to prepare meat for the next days' meals. I also worked a 10 pm to 12 midnight shift as campus guard to make sure all the buildings were secure.

One day I received a note from Dr. Ted Mercer, my English literature teacher, calling me in for a conference. That conference improved my ability to learn tremendously! Dr. Ted had noticed that I was using only one eye to read and to see, and that the other eye was a "lazy eye." He had my vision tested and then got me new glasses to correct the problem.

Dr. Ted also found that I was a regressive reader, a reader who reread everything in order to understand what was being said. That habit was consuming many hours of my study time. Since I was working an 8-hour day as well as attending classes, I had little time to study and that time was precious. Even though I was getting C's in his classes,

I was not going to succeed as a student with the reading problems I had developed.

Dr. Ted took me out of literature and assigned me to a reading program to learn to read correctly and rapidly with comprehension. It literally changed my life! As a result, I moved from being a C-student to being an A-B student. Additionally, I now had more leisure time to enjoy a social life.

As I now think back and meditate on that experience, I realize that I not only was taking classes and working, but I also was finally learning. I felt grateful that Bob Jones College, now Bob Jones University, prepared me for life and success academically. I went on to graduate and earned a Masters in Religious Education, a Masters of Divinity, and a Ph. D. in Counseling Psychology.

When I was 17, BJC required that each ministerial student engage in some kind of ministerial work. So my first summer home, Pastor Gordon arranged with a community church in Yorktown Heights for me to preach on Sundays. A Quaker group ran the church. Early each Sunday morning I would meet with the Quakers. I enjoyed their format. We would come together in a circle and practice complete silence with our eyes closed. I enjoyed the silence. When one of the elders was moved by the spirit, he would speak, asking questions about a matter that was of concern. Then each person would reply. After a few minutes of sharing ideas, we entered into another time of quiet. Then, if one of the members wanted to comment on an issue, he would do so, followed by another open discussion. The elder would ask, "Are we agreed on our plan? If so, I will appoint two of you to work on it and report next week."

It was an experience that opened my mind to studying Quakerism. One of the members gave me a small book to read. I then realized that I was receiving guidance from the group. What were discussed were problems that I could address in the sermons.

I grew in spiritual understanding as I associated with the wise elders and their families. I would eat lunch with a different family each week and really looked forward to it.

It was my introduction to two important concepts: the first, inward wisdom with outward piety; the second, the concept of work as a service to others.

During the week, I had a job with a construction company doing a variety of jobs.

The next year as a sophomore at BJC, I worked on the stage crew building sets for the school drama productions and operas.

Muriel, my friend from church, came to college in 1945. The summers of 1946 and 1947, I traveled with a group to conduct tent meetings in the South. For two summers I experienced doing "tent' revival meetings throughout Tennessee and Alabama.

One summer the Salvation Army sponsored us. I soon found I was getting a broad understanding of Southern style religion. It included plenty of good gospel music, Biblical-centered sermons, and a definite understanding of the great division between the black and white people in the South. It was my first introduction to the lack of equality among people in 1947.

Dr. Glen Tingly of Birmingham, Alabama, was a radio preacher. He enlisted BJC men to conduct tent revival meetings in small rural area villages. He provided the tent as well as a black man to travel with us by truck to set up the tent for one week in each town. We had a few days off to travel. Another student, Elwood Hauser, a musician and saxophonist, had joined me. He led the singing and conducted morning classes for children.

I enjoyed preaching the Gospel. I practiced preaching positive, encouraging messages that brought in full houses. I discovered that I did not want to preach old fashioned "fire and brimstone" sermons. However, many people came to me and said, "We enjoy your approach because most preachers down here are hard-core fundamentalists. Your sermons are different."

I enrolled in Eastern Baptist Theological Seminary in Philadelphia, PA. I majored in Christian Education, obtaining a masters degree in religious education. At the same time, I took all the courses I could in psychology, a field that interested me enormously.

During my 2nd year, I had to write my master's thesis. I decided on the topic of "Role Playing as a Method of Teaching." Role Playing is based on Psychodrama and is still used in the treatment of post-traumatic shock disorder.

Muriel and I decided that we would get married during the Christmas break on December 24th, 1948. We spent our honeymoon in Washington D.C. I thought we had made a good decision since we both had deep love and our goals in life were the same. When issues came up, we went into counseling with Dr. C. Roody, a teacher at EBTF. We both grew as a result of the counseling.

One of the things that I discovered during this period was my deep desire to become a counselor. I had a difficult time convincing the committee of my choice for my master's thesis. I had been studying Dr. Moreno's work with psychodrama at a hospital where he demonstrated the technique on soldiers with Post-Traumatic Stress Disorder. I found the work to be interesting and successful.

The committee finally accepted my version after I changed the title to "Role Playing as a Method of Christian Education." I developed a model to use role-playing as a method for dealing with and solving psychological problems of religious persons. At this time I was an avid reader of both Paul Tournier, a Swiss physician, and Elton Trueblood, a Quaker.

Dr. Tournier's books, *The Meaning of Persons* and *Guilt and Grace,* opened up for me the practice of psychotherapy in conjunction with the Christian faith. He gave me a map for pastoral counseling. He founded the Oxford Group based on his interest in medicine, counseling, and spiritual values. Man, to him, was a spiritual being with a mind, which makes Man a person. He aided me to see that there was a deep spiritual power in practicing psychotherapy.

Elton Trueblood wrote the book, *The Company of the Committed,* that I also found helpful in my learning.

Later on in Chicago, I had the privilege of a one-on-one conversation with Dr. Trueblood after he lectured on the subject of Christian Fellowship. At the end of our talk, he advised, "I want to give you a sentence to carry with you wherever you go—You have more power than you know!" I have kept that sentence as a mantra.

After graduation in June of 1950, I went home to Peekskill, NY, and experienced the week of all weeks! On June 11, 1950, I was ordained as a minister! On June 13, 1950, our son Michael Jr. was born! On June 20, 1950, I was called to be the full-time minister of the Farmer's Mill Community Church, near Carmel, New York.

I was excited when I finally conducted my first wedding ceremony. However, the groom was even more excited. He fainted! Fortunately, my first baptism went more smoothly. It was an outdoor baptism in Lake Bollard.

In 1951 I was called to be Minister of Education of the First Baptist Church of Keokuk, Iowa. I had majored in religious education, and the position sounded like a challenge.

We lived there a year. During that time, we experienced two significant floods with major damage done to the surrounding land. We loved the people of Keokuk, but I was concerned about the flooding and decided to move my family out of the area.

I was soon called to be the full-time Pastor of the First Baptist Church in Sunnyside, Washington, where I served from 1952 to 1955. Our daughter Cynthia was born February 10, 1953.

While Pastor of the church in Sunnyside, several events inspired me to reevaluate whether or not I could stay in the pastoral ministry.

I was invited by one of the members to go deer hunting in upper Idaho near the Canadian Border on the Twisp River. He was an avid and successful world game hunter. It seemed a great way to see the area and to meet people in the group. The caravan consisted of a four-wheel drive truck carrying necessary camping equipment such as gas, food, and water, an enclosed army surplus Jeep, a travel van, and a truck with a winch in the front and rear.

We arrived like a combat troop, setting up camp with military efficiency. I was impressed! The fall weather was mild with hardly any breeze to rustle the leaves. The night sky was black with sparkling stars above us. The forest was filled with the soft rustling of leaves and animal noises. It was a wonderful adventure.

Our first morning was bright and crisp. Breakfast was delicious out in the wilderness. The food and coffee tasted exceptionally good.

We divided into teams of two and set off on different trails carrying guns, ammo, rations, water, and small flashlights.

My partner was a marksman, a seasoned hunter, and the son of the leader. His instructions to me were brief and to the point—"Do Not Talk!"

About 11 am, we were crouched down in the bushes looking out at the tall grass. We got our first view of wildlife as a large buck walked to the edge of the meadow, browsing as he went. My partner gave me the sign to take the shot. I had the deer in the eyepiece and was ready to pull the trigger. At that moment, the buck lifted his head looked into my eyes. I could not shoot! I signed my partner to take the shot. He did. The deer leaped in shock and fell dead. We dressed it out and made a travois, taking the deer back to camp. While our guides cut the deer into parts, I walked out of camp. I had decided never to kill another animal. I took out my 90mm camera and rolls of film to do my shooting after that by taking pictures of the wilderness.

That day, the team killed three more large mule deer. We enjoyed fresh deer steak with roasted corn for dinner that night.

The next day, I was teamed up with the leader D, his young teenage son, and a guide. By mid-morning, we sighted a large black bear and a young cub. The bear and cub turned, saw us, and vanished to our right. Dale called a halt. He whispered, "Bears often go around and track the hunters from the rear." He told us to lean against trees, looking to the front and the rear. Suddenly, the bear reappeared, running toward us from the rear with the cub close behind. Dale took two shots and killed them both. They dropped like rocks, making no sound. That quickly their lives were gone. The hunters were high with excitement. The joy of killing was on their faces and in the voices of the other members of the group. I took more pictures.

Then we broke up into two groups. We were walking up a rise when I suddenly heard a wheezing, buzzing sound breezing by my left ear! I instinctively hit the ground. It was the sound of a gunshot. Dale yelled at his son and walked up to him, put out his hands, and took the rifle. I was alive, but I could still hear that buzzing sound in my ear, remembering the bullet that nearly hit me. I still dream about it.

When we arrived back at camp, we realized that our elderly member was not there. It was late afternoon, and beginning to snow. We spread out in teams of two, walking twenty feet apart in each direction. It was dark when we finally saw the flashlight of one of the groups. They had found Mr. Dow collapsed against a tree, totally disoriented. We helped him back to camp. By then the snow had become heavy, and we knew we must pack up and sleep in the vehicles that night. At dawn, we would start home.

Later as I mused about my experience, I realized that I was in touch with an amazing insight into life. Life is very beautiful, but it can all too quickly, all too suddenly, be ended by death.

Chapter 7
SEEKING WITH AN OPEN MIND

Harlow Willard was my best friend at that time and a fellow minister. He and I each had supportive wives and two children. My wife Muriel was working for an attorney at that time, Mr. Salvanie.

Both Harlow and I were seekers. Together we examined our early belief systems, poking holes in Calvinism and fanatical factions of religions. Of course, we did not broadcast these dialogues, but we were stretching our minds and souls beyond our seminary training. We also enjoyed many fishing trips together on the Columbia and White Rivers, giving us time to discuss our ideas.

One day, Harlow's wife called me. Harlow was taken to the mental ward of a hospital in Yakima, WA. I hurried to the hospital. He was having hallucinations and had undiagnosed schizophrenia. Since he had been put on medication, he was somewhat able to communicate. He shared with me that for the last month he could not preach. As he started towards the pulpit each Sunday, he began to cramp and became violently ill.

I returned the next day. He was somewhat lucid and shared with me his mood swings that he had never shared with anyone before. I knew it was my ignorance of psychology that made me unaware and naive about what he was experiencing. In so many words he had tried to tell me, but I had just failed to comprehend.

I was distressed and shared what had happened with Dr. Russell Orr, our area minister. He obtained a scholarship for me to go to the conference for American Baptist Ministers on Ministry Evangelism at Grew Lake, Wisconsin, the American Baptist Conference Center.

Two of the ministers and I drove to Green Lake. We were all going through questions and major adjustments. I understood but was of little help, reinforcing my desire to become a therapist. I decided on a plan to work in a parish and attend graduate school for my Ph.D.

On the first day of the conference, I heard the ABC speaker, Curtis Nims, speak of his evolution from a near-death experience and alcoholism to becoming an Evangelist. He was also vice president of the Northern Baptist Theological Seminary. I made an appointment with him to seek his advice. At our appointment, he introduced me to John Lavender, minister of the Morgan Park Baptist Church in Chicago, Illinois. He was also a conference speaker on training people to do evangelism in a program called, "Winsome."

When John Lavender's part of the program was over, he invited me to come to Chicago to work with him as his Christian Education and Youth minister. He was willing for me to attend the Northern Baptist Theological Seminary and also work as his assistant.

I met with the Executive Board and they offered me the position. They also wanted Muriel, my wife, to be the church secretary. At that point, Muriel did not know anything about the possible changes. When I called her, I asked her if she wanted the job as church secretary. After she got over the shock, she said, "Sure, but what will you do?" So I told her. She was delighted, so the decision was made to move to Chicago.

Since I already had a master's degree in religious education, I was permitted to do a one-year program for a Master's of Divinity in Counseling and Theology. I also took seminars in psychology at the University of Chicago. I was privileged to be in two seminars for credit in Contemporary Theology and Psychology. I attended seminars with Dr. Carl Rogers, Rollo May, and other theologians. All were liberal and brilliant! I was in a conservative seminary and a liberal university at the same time. The experience broadened my mind, enriched my psyche, and brought me greater mental maturity.

Two significant experiences shaped my future. The first occurred while I was traveling on an elevated train to class one morning. I read an excellent article in the Chicago newspaper by Dr. Melvin Evans, founder of Democracy in Action. He was also the Vice President of Illinois Gas and Electric.

I wrote a thank you note on a postcard to Dr. Evans, complimenting him on the great article on human development that combined spirituality with sound psychology. Much to my surprise, he responded with a four-page letter thanking me for thanking him! He invited me to his seminars for businessmen who were searching for a more balanced life. He became my mentor. Before leaving Chicago, he gave me what became for me a lifetime mantra.

"Michael, you are preparing today and every day for the career you will have tomorrow!" Those words made great sense to me, and I still follow that mantra today.

The second experience was a soul shift for me. I met weekly with Curtis Nims, John Lavender, and Gus Hintz, the pastor of North Shore Baptist Church. We read the book by Thomas Kelley, A Testament of Devotion. We meditated daily and observed weekly what we were experiencing. We also met with Dr. Elton Trueblood, author of books about the Society of Friends, the Quakers. In a private meeting with me, Dr. Trueblood conferred a blessing, "You have more power than you now know!"

I kept up the practice of meeting with other seekers who would sit with me in silently in meditation.

Dr. John Lavender was the most fluent preacher I had experienced in my life. He wrote, or rather dictated, each sermon in full while his wife typed it out on Friday morning. He memorized it over Friday and Saturday. His favorite sermon was called "A Young Man Dreamed a Dream."

Finally, after nearly three happy, successful years, I was ready to move on.

Dr. Curtis Nims recommended me to the First Baptist Church of Arcata, California, at Humboldt University. The head of the pulpit committee was Dr. Dale Turner, who was vice president of Humboldt University. I applied, and was called to be senior minister. I was pastor from July 1958 through July 1966.

Chapter 8

CHANGE AND NEW GOALS

While in Arcata, I spent a great deal of time musing. Mentors had come into my life and influenced me in a new direction. Eventually, I would make a major shift in my life from pastor to psychotherapist, but the time was not quite right.

I was enrolled at Humboldt University, majoring in clinical psychology, and planning to earn a master's degree. I became a licensed MFT (No. 2908) so I could begin counseling. I was among the first 3,000 people in the state of California to be licensed as an MFT.

In the church, I formed many small groups to study and practice prayer, holistic thinking, and meditation. I met Dr. William Parker, who wrote the book, Prayer Can Change Your Life. I used his books with a group who were seeking mental, emotional, and spiritual healing. This led me to know Dr. Cecil Osborn, the founder of the "Yoke Fellowship Groups" in his church. He led an open house program for men who were on parole. Serendipitously, he became a wealthy man. He made several trips to the Holy Land and collected money by selling artifacts. When I asked him how he became rich, he jokingly said, "Not by being a pastor!" He proceeded to teach me to invest in real estate. I started by making friends with successful realtors and attorneys. We also formed a new church in McKinleyville, California, called the Church of the Light.

I used my newfound knowledge to help the church to buy surrounding property for a small down payment. The balance of the money for the property was paid as we divided the land and sold parcels. The proceeds for land we sold for the church were used to pay for our new Educational Building. I also started a day-care center and kindergarten for disadvantaged students.

I bought a choice lot for my family, where I built a beautiful redwood home with four bedrooms and two and a half baths. When I sold the house years later, I made over 60 percent profit.

Those who came for our program eventually became members of the church. I had applied the principle of "serve them and they will come."

I also started doing counseling for several hours a week, which was a dynamic outreach for serving our community. I was privileged to develop an association with several ministers to work with the courts to provide counseling for couples going through divorce. One judge went so far as to tell couples he would not grant them separation until they first went to counseling to see if their problems could be solved!

My desire to be a counselor was increasing. I went to an Ashram with Dr. E. Stanley Jones, a former missionary to India. He was my first model of a deeply dedicated minister who was able to combine psychological concepts and spiritual growth. At my last Ashram, I had a private session with Dr. Jones. He tutored me in the concept of "growing spiritually." At the end of the session, we knelt and Dr. Jones placed one hand on my head and one on my shoulder. We quietly mused and meditated in silence. I felt free of the false and limiting beliefs that had accumulated in my subconscious mind. It was like a warm energy flowing through my whole body. I felt bathed in light. Then Dr. Jones prayed, "Let this young man be a healer of minds, of bodies, and of souls. Amen."

While I was still minister of the First Baptist Church in Arcada, CA, a member of the church was Mr. Bill Thomas who owned two mortuaries. Paul, who became my good friend, was the mortician. As pastor, I was called upon to perform memorial services for families. I often counseled the family members as well as doing the funeral services. I had only done three or four funeral services, but I had the right books and sample services to serve as my map.

Soon I was doing services almost weekly and often found myself dealing with death and dying. I was not psychologically nor spiritually prepared to cope with so many grieving people. It became a crisis for me, so I reached out to professionals in that field for guidance and counseling. The first teacher told me that I first had to face my own mortality in order to develop a deep empathy for others.

I developed greater empathy and stopped being just a professional. Instead, I became a teacher and spiritual healer to those who were depressed, angry, or grieving. In essence, I matured mentally and spiritually.

Three other ministers and I met in a weekly group. We met to study and experience the power of silence. We basically followed the ancient teachings that formed the basis of Quakerism! As I prepared sermons, I changed them into a more metaphorical and meditative form. I also started many group experiments in the church, leading members to spiritual maturity.

One day after a funeral service, Paul asked me if he could talk with me. We went in his office and he shared tearfully that he had been diagnosed with cancer. It had already metastasized to the point that treatment would not help.

Paul said, "I have been a sympathetic person with and for all the families I have served. But I realized, after listening to you and how you have changed over the time we have worked together, that I want you, not my pastor, to be my minister."

I was stunned. I was not prepared for the shock of Paul's imminent death. He had become one of my closest friends. I asked Paul what his spiritual state was. He answered, "I have been a good Lutheran all of my life, but I am not a Christian. I want to become a Christian, and have you baptize me by immersion."

I made an appointment for Paul to spend a morning with me in my office. I led Paul through two steps. The first step was to accept and experience what the Bible teaches about being born again. The second was the opening of his mind and spirit to spiritual teaching. The next day, I baptized him by immersion.

Every day we talked on the phone. He said, "Thanks for being here when I need you. I am now okay and ready for what is next."

Within a few weeks, he died. He requested my presence with his family. His Lutheran pastor officiated at a family meeting at the church.

As I contemplated, I knew that I was called to be there and serve Paul. I was then thinking about becoming a full-time psychotherapist and no longer being a pastor of a church. However, there was a plan waiting for me that postponed my goal until 1973.

A few weeks later, I called my mentor, Dr. Russell Orr, who was now our State Executive minister for the American Baptist Churches. I had counseled with Dr. Orr and told him Arcata was my last perish. He understood. I told him I wanted to leave the pastoral ministry, study for a Ph. D., and become a full-time therapist. During our appointment, Dr. Orr said, "I have a place in mind for you that will allow you to do both—study for a Ph. D. program and be a minister to a church at the same time." Then he said, "What if you take a small church in Livermore where the climate is warmer but better for your daughter Dawn? The Church Extension mission will pay you the same salary you are now receiving. You could attend the Baptist Seminary and work on your doctorate as part of the contract. However, let me tell you that the church is in a crisis and has no funds."

I agreed but decided that I had better do some demographic research, and not go down a blind alley.

I discovered that it was a small church with only 25 active members. The building was a rather shabby, old chapel from Camp Parks in Pleasanton that would seat no more than 100 people. The carpet was well worn, and the whole inside and outside of the building needed painting. Still I felt, "I can't lose! It can only get better!" In May of 1976, I was called to be the pastor.

I decided ahead of time to structure the leadership so that I would be Chairman and Executive Minister. I knew that I needed to be a strong leader or nothing would get done without a hassle. I shared this with the church members, and they agreed. I started by saying, "I won't preach my first sermon until we organize a crew to clean up the church. We can seek others to help, asking family and friends."

The First Goal: Paint the whole building inside and out; fix the noisy water cooler-air conditioner that rattles and leaks.

The Second Goal: Install new carpet and refurbish the sanctuary; put a new finish on the pulpit.

The Third Goal: Cut the grass all around the buildings; clear the waist-high weeds on the rear lot.

The Fourth Goal: Repaint and repair one of the classrooms; re-carpet my office and conference room.

The Fifth Goal: Fix and update the First Baptist Church sign in front.

We did it all! Morale in the congregation jumped from 0 to 100 percent. The women were ecstatic to put up curtains and new drapes.

The members also agreed that I would be permitted to work on a doctoral program with the blessings of Dr. Ron, our American Baptist Church area Minister.

Without bragging now, I set out then to be a creative, forceful, loving Pastor. I made it clear that if they could not accept strong leadership, they should step aside and not be a hindrance, even if it meant their leaving the church.

The first step was to persuade them to sell a property outside of town that they wanted to someday build on. I already had a site in town in mind. I needed a green light to put together a program to purchase the new site and plan for its utilization.

The plan was to put down a $100 deposit and pay off the site by selling the out-of-town property, rent out two houses that were on the property, and immediately build a functional, multi-use building to hold Sunday services. We met in the large open area for worship and used the small rooms for Sunday school. During the week, we sponsored a day-care center called "The Gingerbread House."

My goal was accomplished by setting aside three acres of the nine-acre parcel to be sold. My plan was to divide the three acres into a nine-house subdivision. I would keep one site to build my own house on. I engaged architect

Randall Schlintz to plan and develop the future of Pepper Tree Place. He bought one site and I sold 7 other sites to be built on. The proceeds from the sale went to the church building fund.

The next steps were to sell the parsonage on Hillcrest Avenue. I would move out when my new home on Pepper Tree Place was finished.

The church made enough money to pay off the site, engage the architect, and build a new sanctuary. My plan had worked! When I preached my first sermon in the new church, it not only was full, but we had to add seats in the back.

The goal for the First Baptist Church of Livermore, CA, was to be debt free! Needless to say, the congregation was overjoyed when we were able to accomplish our dream. By then, we had over 250 members.

The encouragement of my mentors, my planning, plus musing, brought forth the dream. Nothing happens in a vacuum. By the way, the church won an architectural award by the A.I.A for the new church. We all celebrated the honor.

Chapter 9

STARTING OVER

From there we bought the best site in Livermore to build a children's day school. We grew to 250 members within four years. We were happy with what had been accomplished. Then my life changed enormously.

Muriel and I had some difficulties along the way. We were in the bedroom arguing over a check for $500 that she had written and signed using my name. The bank knew us and cashed it. She at first denied it, then started to walk away angrily. With the back of my hand, I tapped her buttock. She reacted with rage and walked into the living room to sit on the couch. The children were not home.

She announced, "I don't love you and I haven't for 20 years! I don't want us to be husband and wife; however, we can stay together, but live our own lives."

I was stunned. We had argued before about how her spending was keeping us in debt regardless of how much we made. She was as cold as stone.

All of a sudden, I sobbed. I left the house crying. She made no effort to stop me. I walked in the dusk, crying my heart out and sobbing out loud. I was so distraught that I felt disoriented. I stopped at every house that had sprinklers going and soaked my head and face. This went on for over an hour. I was finally drained and numb.

I had wandered in a state of distraction. I found myself in a park sitting on a bench for perhaps 30 minutes. A man saw me and asked, "Can I help?"

I said, "Yes. I feel terrible. Could you please take me home?" He drove me home without saying a word. When we arrived, I thanked him and went in the house. Muriel's car was gone. The children were sitting at the kitchen table eating and told me, "Mom had to go back to the office."

I took a shower and dressed and drove to my office at the church. I sat, musing for hours. Finally, I was calm and accepted the reality that she—Muriel my wife—was not going to be my wife any longer. I had to pull myself together to carry out my duties as a Pastor and father. I had to achieve the church's goal of completing our new sanctuary as well as the new house I was building on Peppertree Place.

The next day I did not speak to Muriel. I contacted one of my friends who worked in the Director's Office and shared with him what had happened. I didn't want him to think the changes I would be making were strange. I would need to invest much more of my time and energy on my children and career.

He looked at me quizzically and said, "I understand. I think you ought to know that Muriel and her boss, the Director of Personnel, spend a lot of time together at lunches, meetings, and before and after work. Muriel is totally caught up in the relationship, but I don't think it's sexual. I know you feel betrayed, and I'll help you all that I can."

Then I knew why she was so distant from me. I never confronted her with what I knew. We ceased being intimate, but I treated her with kindness, keeping busy with all the work I had started.

Other lab employees called and said they understood what was going on. They would still be my friend and remain a supporter at the church. I was outwardly the same, but inwardly, I was growing away from Muriel. I filed a document with the bank to stop all credit cards and checking accounts. Then I moved my accounts to a new bank. I placed, with legal guidance, a garnishment on all her wages.

When she approached me about the changes, I put up my hand and said, "Stop! I will give you a generous allowance and make the payment on the house and cars. Otherwise, if you don't want me to play tough, I will make sure you will be out of a job at the lab. She saw a Michael that she had never seen before, as well as the cold look in my eyes and on my face. She agreed and signed all the papers I needed.

As I pondered my actions, I knew I could never be the same person. I decided to go to psychotherapy in Berkeley where I was enrolled in a Ph. D. program. It was the beginning of a new phase and a redirection of my life. When I completed all my goals as the Pastor, I would resign and never be a Pastor of a Church again. I would begin a journey for healing, wholeness, and spirituality.

Muriel did not know I knew that she and her boss at the Lab were being transferred to Washington, D.C. to set up a program through the Department of Energy. Therefore, I made sure legally that I would have complete custody of our five children, and they would stay with me until they finished high school. I also made sure Muriel would not gain any value from our house until we arrived at a complete understanding on financial matters.

As I mused, I knew that my first clear goal was to completely forgive Muriel and let her go. The second was to map out my future as a professional. I began a new spiritual journey into wholeness and joy with a deep and profound peace of mind.

During this time, I studied and grew, becoming a master Hypnotherapist and more of a spiritual leader. I discovered psychosynthesis by Dr. Roberto Assagioli, and absorbed his teachings into my life. I studied psychosynthesis at a seminar in London, England.

I took advanced classes in San Francisco, California. I was following the " inner light."

I was further influenced by neurolinguistic programming that I studied with the founders Richard Bandler and John Grindler, from the University of Santa Cruz and Palo Alto. I fully experienced the three "S's" in my meditation: synthesis, synergy, and inner-soul spirituality.

I planned periodic retreats to contemplate and enlarge my spirituality. I attended the Conference of Wholeness at Asilomar. I also attended the Tibetan Seminary, studying Kum Nye, as well as other conferences with many men and women who were also expanding spiritually, using meditation and psychotherapy. I felt my mind and soul expanding beyond religion to a higher state of awareness of others and myself.

As I mused, the fires of purification and wonderment were parallel journeys.

One of the biggest leaps I made was to align myself with a deeply wise author and psychotherapist, Dr. A. H. Almas, author of *The Void* and *The Diamond Approach.*

With many other counselors, we met with Dr. Almas, who shared with us his journey from work as a successful New York psychotherapist to a total invalid from polio living in an iron lung. His journey became a metaphoric transformation.

I entered into my void, musing about that! I saw things in a new light. I was increasingly aware that all my experiences led me to this juncture. I could fall back into an abyss, or I could choose to move forward. All the roles I played were channeled into spending time musing.

At the age of 46 in June of 1973, I resigned as Minister of the First Baptist Church of Livermore. Most people reacted with shock, and a few with joy because they wanted me to move on. I resigned when I followed my own metaphor: "Build a bridge to the next shore and do not jump foolishly into a cold river!"

I was appointed by the Police Department of Livermore to be Executive Director of the Horizons Program founded by the California Council on Criminal Justice. The grant included the cities of Livermore and Pleasanton. I was also continuing to work part-time to become a licensed M.F.T.

As all this was going on, my wife Muriel had left. She went to Washington, D.C., working with her boss Glen in the Department of Energy. She then went to Geneva,

Switzerland, to set up the personnel section for the United States for the S.A.L.T. talks.

I was able to see it in a new light. We were both set free to come out of the cocoon of the past to become butterflies, new persons. All of my experiences melded together, bit by bit, into a new and deeper sense of meaning and purpose.

"As I mused..." became a daily mantra for me, which I experienced at all levels in expanding my spirit. In my musing, I saw myself growing into a new image of a man breaking out of the shadows of the past. The new me was the man inside, manifesting from within the potential that was already there. I realized before I came out of the confined shell that I wanted to please others. I chose to be a compassionate counselor and leader. I had shifted my gears, discovering that serving as pastor from 1950 to June 1973 had taken all my psychic energy and time to be a good minister. Out of meditation, musing, and mastery of my time, I pulled out all the stops and guided my energy into growth and change.

The training that I had taken was food for my soul, my mind, and my expanded consciousness. Academically, I have a B.A. from Bob Jones University, a M.R.E. from Eastern Baptist Theological Seminary, a Master's of Divinity from the Northern Baptist Seminary, graduate courses at the Doctoral level in counseling Psychology,

and a Ph.D. in counseling Psychology from Columbia
Pacific University.

Along the way, I obtained a license as a Marriage Family
Therapist on June 4, 1959. Following is a list of educational
courses I have taken in specialized training to become a
competent and effective therapist.

San Francisco University: Clinical Hypnosis
University of Santa Cruz: S.A.G.E. courses, M.F.T. and
    Hypnosis
Stanford Extension
M.F.T. license from 1959 to 2010
Seminars in imagery and visualization
Studies and training in Psychosynthesis, Robert Assagioli,
    in England and Italy
Certified in 1999 in Critical I Stress Management
Many seminars on drug abuse plus Continuing Education
    classes for M.F.T. license
Member of Clinical Hypnosis Society of the United States
As an ordained minister, I qualify and can serve as a
    Counselor by Professional and Business codes of
    California.

During the 1980s, I was also a licensed Realtor and
worked with several agencies. I worked as a realtor on
Fridays, Saturdays, and Sundays. On Mondays, I took
time off after closing paper work with title companies,
inspectors, and builders. I needed this time to cognitively
read, meditate, and muse.

On Tuesdays, Wednesdays, and Thursdays, I was in the counseling office seeing clients for counseling, marriage and family therapy, and meeting with other therapists for breakfast or lunch. I also consulted with several M.D.s including seeing clients at the Castro Valley Medical Center with Dr. John Turns.

It was at this time that I met Judy. She was a member of a Tai Chi group that I was sponsoring. She was in the process of getting a divorce from her husband, John.

My divorce from Muriel had been final. She had moved to Oakton, Virginia, and was working in Washington, D.C.

Judy was 36 and I was 53 years old. She was an attractive green-eyed, red-haired woman who loved life. She and I went to church together. She was an accomplished pianist and organist. We had many things in common, including music. We were married in 1980.

During our marriage, I was very successful in real estate and we lived in several beautiful homes. Judy worked for the Livermore Lab and enjoyed having many friends. She was the joy of my life, and we did many things together such as traveling, and attending concerts and plays in San Francisco.

Then lightening struck. We were going to East Livermore in my 1984 Volvo. I had stopped at an intersection, looked both ways, and saw no cars coming. I moved forward less than 3 feet when we were struck by a speeding Toyota pickup truck driven by an inexperienced teen-age driver. The pickup crashed into the left side of the Volvo. The impact caved in the whole left side of the car. It tossed me across the car, tearing me out of the safety belt. My head impacted the windshield on the passenger side and cracked the window. Judy was tossed about and had muscular injuries from hitting the right door of the car. The driver behind us called for an ambulance and the police.

For a moment, I was conscious. The attendants, who were sliding a board under my back, heard me ask, "Where are my shoes?" Then I blacked out.

I was taken to the Emergency Room at Livermore Valley Hospital, where after some time I became conscious. My physician, Dr. Mandeville, was concerned. He told me, "Well, it's your back." He asked me to move my feet, but I was unable to. I asked, "Is my back broken?" He replied, "No, but you may have serious spinal injuries and you have lost feeling in your feet."

I thought, "Well, this is it. Will I ever walk again?"

Judy was there and squeezed my hand. She said, "I am with you and things will get better!" It boosted my morale, and I felt tears flowing down my face.

I was placed in a lower body restraint so I wouldn't make sudden movements. Dr. Mandeville told me we didn't know how much damage was done. Several hours later, after many X-rays, MRIs, and a CAT scan, Dr. Mandeville assured me that there was no severance of my spine. It was then that the highway patrol officer came in to question me. His first remark was, "You were lucky you were in a Volvo. In any other car, you would be dead!" Then very professionally, he questioned Judy and me. He told us that the other driver, who had been shaken up badly, was all right. The truck and the Volvo were totaled, however. The young driver was found to be at fault.

I began a year of physical therapy and healing. I was forced to stay home. I could walk, but only with the aid of crutches. I was sent to Eden Hospital in Castro Valley for a specialized spinal test. I was in serious shape with pain and depression. I was beginning to realize that I would never be the same in many ways. What I did not anticipate, however, was that Judy was moving out of our relationship. I simply could not meet her needs any longer, and we had grown apart.

What I discovered was that Judy had been in treatment with a psychiatrist and this event triggered off a complete change in her personality. She left me and moved on to a new relationship. I was not surprised, but I experienced extreme loss and sadness. All of my dreams were gone. I went into individual therapy and group therapy in order to heal.

Later, after Judy was gone and remarried, I called her psychiatrist, Dr. John. I had heard he was leaving his practice to become a priest. We talked. He said, "I can't tell you about anything confidential; however, your ex was diagnosed for severe depression and bipolar disorder."

One of Judy's friends called me to ask if we could meet. She told me Judy had a breakdown, was suicidal, and was in the hospital. I asked her what the admission was for. She replied, "Possible schizophrenia. She was unable to be rational and was under severe stress."

I called Judy's sister in Louisiana. She told me that Judy did have serious mental problems in college and afterwards. She then assured me that Judy thought I had been the best man in her life. Eventually, Judy left Livermore.

I knew I must enter my next stage. He heard my cry! He put a new song in my mouth! As I mused, I found in the Psalms of David that he had been a man like me. He loved music, songs, poetry, metaphors, and nature. As I mused, the fire burned! The burning flame created heat and light. Both are important to a shepherd watching his flocks. Fire is passion. Through musing, we can set the world on fire! Fire cleanses and illuminates impurities. Be on fire for good, joy, and happiness.

As I mused, I became quiet. I had an experience under the power of Psalm 46:10 that reads: "Be still, and know that I am God! Walk in light with God!" I knew that when we have the light, we will speak words of hope in and to a world where there is darkness, depression, and dread. God always hears. He is my Rock. God is a refuge in the midst of stress. Seeing the picture of David and his experiences, I reframed it into my experiences and learned about myself in the process.

Chapter 10

A Mystic Soul Evokes the Muse

I am a metaphorical thinker and a mystic soul as the result of explorations on my spiritual path. Two spiritual revelations jumped out at me. I progressed from these early experiences to a profound, mystical vision that came in a moment of clarity and openness. I have never shared this with anyone till now! I also experienced many intuitive hunches.

While counseling a woman client, she asked me to assist her in solving a problem using hypnosis. I knew her as a very intelligent, capable and caring person, who on the surface did not show her inner feelings.

After a brief introduction, I asked her to regress in five-year segments and let me know what was coming to her conscious mind.

The first five years she saw her relationship with her husband and the dynamics of their experience. She was in a still peaceful state yet clear what she and her husband needed to do to continue together and have a good future life.

Then we regressed to a ten-year span. She was not agitated by the regression. I asked why she was frowning. She replied, "I just saw how complex everything was and how stressful." I inquired, "What do you want in the now to create a less stressful life?"

She relaxed even more and said, "I know what I have to do!"

Suddenly her head dropped forward and she went into a deep trance. I let her continue with the experience to see where she would go with that very deep state.

After a few seconds, she said, "I am in a Temple in Israel. You are the High Priest. You are dressed in the garb of the High Priest and like the High Priest in the past.

"Who am I?" I asked. She opened her eyes and said, "You are the original High Priest of Melchizedek who appeared to Abraham." With that, she suddenly came out of the trance. I asked if she remembered any part. She said, "No, but I know I had an image of you."

We closed the session because she told me she was okay and knew what her intuition was teaching her. She knew what she needed to do!

After she left, I sat quietly and meditated on what the vision meant and what I was going to do. I did not have a

Bible in the office, so I went home and read Hebrews 3, 4, and 5.

Like a neon light flashing on my mental screen, I was aware of the following: You are a Priest. You will form an order after the model of Jesus as a Priest after the order of Melchizedek, Hebrew 7:21. I had been called to live by faith and serve others as a priest/healer. It took me several weeks of musing, meditating, and wondering to create a new pattern for life.

Another verse that became a mantra for me was John 13:13. "God is love" became the basis for my theology. Everything I do is based on these words! I am a priest, after the order of Melchizedek. God is love and I am His servant-priest. I show that love as a psychotherapist-healer.

We must develop a core within us to learn how to cogitate, how to imagine, and how to meditate—our inner sanctum of love. Another Bible verse is the corner stone of my experience, Galatians 2:20. To paraphrase, it is all in the inner sanctum of my being. I am called to quietly serve as a healer of body, mind, and spirit.

People who came into my life who fit into this idea, I invited to join me in the order of Melchizedek. We do not have meetings, but we simply serve in our unique way. I chose to follow an intuitive idea and wrote letters of appreciation to others who I knew were serving humankind in their own compassionate way. I will not publish that list, but I will share these two names from it—Sister Mother Theresa and Dr. Billy Graham. My soul soaks up warm vibrations when I think of those who are servants of God.

Perhaps you can use some of the following methods that I have used to "muse." I truly know that if you do, the light will also come to you.

In Faye Kellerman's book, Straight Into Darkness, a detective known as Bang was pondering about a criminal who was killing people. Bang suddenly experienced a solution. He repeated, "It creatively sprang from musings deep in my subconscious." It was from that very place that the idea came to him just as deep musing could also lead each of us if we learn how to muse and practice it daily. When we see solutions, it all comes together.

I shared earlier my conversion experience. I stated that it was a mystical experience. I saw the light. It happened at a religious conference. I did not compute nor think about being a Christian at the time. I was in communion with Christ who entered my heart and mind. I saw the light of where my behavior was leading me and decided to give my life, body, and soul to be in that light.

However, I wanted more than "Churchianity." I had already seen that didn't work too well for me. All the roles I played were channeled so that I could spend time musing.

As I now mused, the fire burned more brightly and hot! I experienced a burning of the dark part of the spectrum of feelings of being cleansed and healed of all remorse from the past.

Now musing is as natural as breathing to me. The ways of using the quality of musing can change the now into a day-by-day peaceful state.

I want to expand the powerful role women played in my life to teach me to love. In the now, I would like to share some of these soul discoveries I adapted into my inner being.

On July 10, 1993, I married the love of my life, Diane Jean. We have created a great life with each other. I had learned to love from Muriel, 1930s to her death; from Judy, 1980 to 1986, a roller coaster; and of course from Diane J, my present wife, love, and best friend.

I want to share with you all that came out of pain and loss and my transformation into a new person, with the help of many great teachers, loving friends, and God.

"As I mused" became a daily mantra, which I experienced at all levels in expanding my spirit.

It was during this time of major adjustments that I set aside time at home to "muse." As I mused, the door of my imagination was opened to see new ways of serving my clients. I could see and hear some of their inner requests that were not spoken directly to me but to which they only hinted.

Underneath the problems that brought them into therapy was a need for us to talk heart to heart. I took time to meditate before each session, taking moments to interpret their inner needs that were not spelled out clearly as they talked.

I asked my "muse" to open my inner wise self to respond to their inner vibrations. I also felt more empathy and clearness as to how to analyze and answer their needs. Some of their inner thoughts were filled with hurt and anger.

When I discovered from Psalm 39 that I was a muser, I found the quote that opened my mystic metaphorical side. It was, "As I mused, the fires burned." Now I was more centered and compassionate! I was a more effective therapist and successful realtor. I was preparing then who I would be in my tomorrows.

I was still working as a realtor and counseling. I spent as much time in Berkeley with a group that I was associated with called Melia. In that group I met Dr. A. H. Almas, a psychiatrist. I went into intensive group therapy with several other therapists who had also experienced serious traumas and grief.

Dr. Almas led us to see that we had to enter our "void" before we could be healed. His method was called, "The Diamond Approach." I followed his therapy and was able to create a new life and direction. It was a time of personal change and deepening spirituality. Then in therapy, I discarded all the old, dysfunctional beliefs and attitudes that I could at the time.

I found myself opening the door to compassion of my clients' inner pain, most of which came from their childhood and early adolescence. Interestingly, I found us, clients and I, creating a bond with healing that's for the here and now. They also released pent-up resentments that were not on the surface and in no way related to the presenting problem. I heard and responded.

I had recently completed advanced training in E.M.D.R. I found that by using a non-directive approach I could lead them by asking them gently but firmly to inwardly say the words, "I'm letting that go." Needless to say, my clients showed me their thankfulness for helping them relieve their inner pain from the past.

As I mused, the fire of imagination and wisdom created greater effectiveness on my part and more healing in my clients.

Diane and I decided to move on and sell the Danville property. We searched for over a year for a place to move that was right for us. Serendipitously, things began to open up that we could not have foreseen.

The right property became available in Corral De Tierra in the Monterey area. Diane and I were of one mind that this was the place for us. However, we reached a stalemate on the price. We were stretching our limits and the owners were stuck on their asking price. We backed away and turned the matter over to the universe. "If it was right for us, then something would make it possible!"

As I mused, I found clarity and peace of mind that we were on the right track and that we just had to surrender our efforts and wait.

A couple of weeks later, the owner's wife called me and said, "We will accept your offer."

I asked her gently, "What happened to help you decide?"

She replied, "I am a faithful Episcopalian, and I learned you were on the Episcopal Church roster as a Eucharistic Priest in the Livermore Church. The next day, our attorney called us and informed us that my grandmother wanted me to have her estate and funds. She is going into a retirement home. I inherited a large sum of money and her million-dollar house in the heart of Monterey, where I want to live! So I want you to have the Corral house to live in."

Wow! We had the home and property of our dreams in an area where I could set up a private practice. So we moved to Corral de Tierra on a three-acre wooded site. The land backed up to 20 acres of scenic land on which no one could build. Diane and I sold our properties and pooled our resources to pay cash for our new home.

So from 1999 till now, I have been on an exciting, spiritual journey. I started in a small office in Salinas, but set my sights on an office on Garden Road in Monterey. Eventually, a clinical Psychiatrist rented her room to me one day per week. Events transpired with her practice and she then decided to release the office to me while she rented an office across the hall for one day per week.

My dreams were coming true. I found myself making notes to write a book. Writing a book had never entered my conscious mind before, but it became important to me.

Then again Life intervened! Everything started to change enormously about 3 years ago. It became a trial of my faith forced by circumstances. I found I could no longer practice as a therapist. I had three minor accidents with my new Jaguar. Although I rationalized the accidents were not my fault, I knew something serious was happening to my body and reactions. I had always relied on my logic to get me up and to start me over when things got difficult. This was different.

One evening, I was coming from my office on Route 68 to my home during a heavy rainstorm. Suddenly, a large dog ran out of a driveway in front of my car. Because of what was slowly happening to my body, I could not take my foot off the accelerator to hit the brakes! I swerved into the oncoming traffic instead. It was now dusk and I could see the headlights of the oncoming cars. I swerved more to the left automatically to avoid a head-on collision. I hit the ditch on the left and flipped over to the right side of the car, scraping a path for thirty or more feet before stopping. I was suddenly hanging upside down still in my seat belt.

A man tapped on my sunroof window. I hit the button and was amazed that the sunroof window opened. He asked, "Can you talk?"

I answered, "Yes."

He replied, "I called the police and ambulance and they are on the way. Stay put! You may be more injured than you know!" He stayed with me and talked to me. I asked him to call Diane and tell her what happened. I was going to request that I go to CHOMP, the Community Hospital of Monterey Peninsula. He did call Diane just before the police arrived. One came to my window and knocked. I pushed the button and the window came down. His first question was, "Have you been drinking?"

I laughed and answered, "I never touch the stuff!"

He said, "Good! Help is here!" Then the ambulance drivers came in a back door and slipped a board under me, strapping me to it before releasing the seat belt. I was in the hands of three gentle men as they opened my door and eased me out. The man who first talked to me told them I wanted to go to CHOMP.

I was soon in the emergency room being attended to by a doctor, prepping me for a CAT scan of my neck and shoulders. The doctor let us know that my neck was not broken, but that I had some "funny quirks" in my neck. He attributed the quirks to a former accident.

The doctor was very Irish and had a great sense of humor. He put me in a neck brace and asked me to stay in the ER for observation until he felt I was over the shock.

I was in a great deal of pain and discomfort. Needless to say, I went into treatment. The ER doctor recommended that I see a Neurologist to track down what was going on with my reflexes.

I went to a neurologist who put me through a thorough exam. He answered, "Michael, you have Peripheral Neuropathy. You must not drive your car again." It was difficult, but I gave Diane my car keys.

I didn't know what Peripheral Neuropathy was but researched it from all angles. I had to go to physical therapy and because of circumstances, went to a new neurologist, Dr. A. Centurion, my current treatment physician.

Because of these problems, I had to retire my practice. I continued to see my clients in a home office.

I read and reread Psalm 39. It became my map. I began a soul journey based on David's example of musing. I had been practicing this form of meditation, but now it took on a new meaning. Then I read Psalm 40 as God's reply to Psalm 39.

I knew the accident would require the first step to a whole new life. I had no idea what that entailed; however, I had faith and hope. I wondered what would happen and what the path would be into the future. I let the experience sit in the back part of my brain.

Now I muse on wisdom, seeing, love, light, energy, wholeness, and joy. "No matter what happens to throw you off center, come back wiser than ever!"

Also, I knew my dreams would change. Therefore, I will share my dreams as a step toward musing.

PART II

THE SEVEN KEYS TO
SPIRITUAL ENLIGHTENMENT

Chapter 11
KEY I   SYMBOLS, DREAMS, AND INTERPRETATIONS

Here are some notes I made on the mornings following each dream. I will not interpret the dreams, but let the story or meaning come to you. I often mull over a conflict thinking about what actions to take.

Dream on a Tuesday:

Diane and I were walking through a large department store. Diane was walking ahead. I stopped and was talking to a person about a purchase. As I looked forward, Diane was way out in front and suddenly turned left. I followed, but no Diane. I turned in another direction and Diane was exiting the building. The exit door was closing slowly. When I went out the door, Diane was gone. I woke. She was still in bed sleeping deeply. I dozed, asking myself questions. Was I now afraid that Diane would leave me?

I went back to sleep. A man appeared. He said, "I am a Master Teacher. Life is like a game of billiards. Each day, you break the formation of the billiard balls. It's not preset. You can't predict the variables. It's all how you play the game." I went back into a deep delta sleep.

I dreamed of a flood. A voice said, "You don't know how to escape, so ask for help. Start at the bottom of the problem. Be humble. You don't know it all." I woke and went to my office and wrote down what I had dreamed.

The next night, I reviewed the dream. The Teacher appeared and said to me, "Time is in the process of being gone. It never was. It's forever gone. There is no going back to what never was!" I mused about the dreams, and realized that life is illusion. Living is now! You are the architect of your own life. Discover your dreams. Then draw your plans and remodel your life!

I dreamed that a Jewish woman received a letter from her boyfriend. It said, "I'm afraid of letting go. I am feeling your love and experience my passion. But you are like a shallow pond of water. It's safe but has no depth. However, I'm somewhat glad, because I have a fear of being caught in ocean tides and crashing waves."

She replied, "I have waited for you, but I won't wait for much longer. I want us to jump in the ocean and experience its depths, feel our love like a fire mixed with passion and fear. By being afraid of losing me, you will! Experience the ocean's overwhelming power of love. Pools are limpid. Oceans are alive and dynamic. Love me the way you can and let go of playing everything safe. Love me passionately and I'll love you back. Be jealous but not obsessive. Love me fully and fulfill your possibility of joyousness."

Please note that I had asked my subconscious to reveal to me the root of pain.

"I'm uptight, and holding on, and afraid. So the dream spoke!"

Dream: I was on a boat. I am a child. I felt that no one was listening. I hear funny noises and said so. Adults said: "You are imagining it. There is nothing wrong." So I put my ear to the deck. There were groans and cracking sounds. I went below and saw that it was flooded. I ran up and sounded the alarm to get off the ship.

We left, but it was too late. The ship sank and very little was salvaged. I looked for my mom, but she was not in my rescue boat. She went with others and wouldn't come back. Another child comforted me as I was groaning. I wished the others and I had listened to the signs, but now it was too late.

I fell asleep dreaming of the ocean. A man who looked like a prophet appeared shouting, "I will give you what you don't have! Eat, drink, and be merry for tomorrow we die."

I replied, "I wasn't full and felt empty. I miss enjoyment. I am afraid to live and enjoy people and things. I fear happiness."

God came in with laughter and joy. He led us to an open circle in the woods. There was a banquet table.

Eat! It may be your last meal. Eat, drink, and be merry and be happy now! If you die tomorrow you will die joyfully and peacefully. I will give you what you don't have!

Then out of my memory came a voice. "Give what you have. You already have nuts, so I give you dates"

Let's stop to reflect how to interpret dreams.

First, I see dreams as stories or parables written by us in symbols! The images give meaning to our lives. We have an inner self, and by following the light, we find meaning in our lives.

It's known that we have two levels of sleep: non-REM and REM, or rapid eye movement. REM evokes images, stories, and scenes. Shakespeare said, "Dreams knit up the raveled sleeve of care." Dreams mirror that which is going on inside us physically. I believe that metaphorically our deep self is most open to listen to the Divine or the God of Light.

I encourage my readers to record dreams in a journal upon waking. Later, interpret dreams using intuition. Free associate. I do urge you to use caution though. Do not judge! Read books about dreaming. Have a trusted person to talk to about what you have experienced.

If our dreams are sensing disturbances, seek out a therapist, an understanding person, or a trained pastoral counselor. By all means, keep it simple!

In 1980, I was married to Judy, but our marriage ended in divorce. That month, I dreamed that Judy and I were riding a tandem bike—side by side. We were riding on country roads, singing spirituals and hymns. One was "Amazing Grace."

Then Judy asked me to baptize her by immersion. She said, "I was baptized as a baby, but I want a spiritual baptism. Then we will go to a church, but the church only allows 17 people to enter."

I woke up and wrote, but the dream was already fading away. It was clear, "Forgive her and those who lead her in a different direction." I realized I had to let her go.

I dreamed I was hiking and riding bikes with a woman friend. She was seeking informal counseling and clearly no sex. Suddenly a man appeared who had been in a car accident. The woman went with him to drive him where he could be helped.

I met another woman friend. We were eating at her house. On the table were blue and red one-quart cartons of milk. We needed food so we went shopping. She met a man and told me she planned an affair. She told me that it's okay for me to do so also. She said, "I am comfortable with that kind of arrangement."

I asked her who was counseling her. She replied, "David. He told me to be okay with having secrets." She left me then to go away with an old friend, but she would not tell me whom it was.

All of these dreams are the whisperings of the subconscious. Something is not right in our lives or the dreams would not end in loss. They are warnings from the subconscious to be aware of what is going on in our lives so that we may seek change to rebalance our relationships.

Our real estate company was facing a trial about a transaction. The night before, I realized my fear and dread of depositions and going to court on fear of punishment. I fell asleep with those thoughts on my mind.

A counselor appeared to me looking like an M.D. friend of mine. He said, "Out of this experience, remember you will recover by using Eye Movement and Thought Field therapy to process out fears. The results will be that you will be calm. Be confident in the truth. Use all your inner tools!"

Two nights later, I woke up at 4 a.m. "Remember your fear of interrogation comes from your father and how unjust he was in his punishment." We went to court and won! After the trial, I became depressed and physically ill with flu-like symptoms. I saw that I had a deep aversion to unfair interrogations.

Two months later, I dreamed that a Sage came to me in Eastern garb. He said, "Do this movement and energy will come." He showed me combinations of Tai Chi, breathing, and Qi Chong.

Then a young woman joined us, and we did the movements. I was excited and felt alive. When I awoke, I made notes and fell back to sleep.

Two hours later, a teacher of Tarot came to me and said, "The cards told me to tell you to fly like a falcon! Follow your intuition. Be centered. You have a crab shell but be in touch with your inner self and be secure."

Now what to make of that?

I woke up early one morning remembering the dream I was having. Dagwood was shouting, "We have no candy to give for Halloween!" Then the kids showed up in a variety of costumed characters with masks.

Blondie went to the door to give them treats like books and toys. Then one of the characters came back with a big bag, dumping all the stuff on the floor. He then marched off! Dagwood looked flummoxed!

It was 2006, and approximately 3:30 a.m. when I woke up from a dream. I was at my desk musing. The fire burned. Then I heard myself speaking. I am contemplating existence and the end of life. Then I heard the words, "Circle of energy and light." My thoughts led to conceptualizing soulness. I saw a tiny dot of light. It was a soul, a Nano-speck of light. It could only be viewed through a microscope. The Nano-lights were the essence of my whole being, past, present, and future. I died with a gentle sigh, letting go with peace and sadness mixed together.

I soon was traveling faster than the speed of light through the Cosmos, conscious of being only energy filled with vibrancy. Time had no relevance nor did space. Only movement through infinity in darkness with lights flashing on and off. Glowing clouds exploded, but they made no sound. It continued on and on. It was timeless, yet I was experiencing movement.

Suddenly, we were Nano-lights traveling, but with immense space between us. I knew we were destined to meet or gather somehow, someplace.

Then before me, I sensed infinitely high clouds of a milky blue essence, where all the Nano-souls were clustering to form a changing cloud-like place!

We moved to the center. I knew that was home. I was safe and serene. The sadness of the early stages was gone. I was reunited with kinder beings, knowing them as Nano-souls. I was in a resting place. We could be there forever not mindful of loss or aloneness. We were one. There was just being.

Then suddenly it was clearing and I could leave in an exalted state of serenity to go back to the earthly plane to be born again. We were in a state of androgyny and yin yang soulness. We would get back in that oneness state.

I did not know or remember oneness, I just remember being a Nano-light soul. I was not aware of time, but I was entering a space, a place where time is existence.

I awakened with a start and hurried to my office to write everything down, worried that I would forget. Now that I read it all over, I think of the words of a famous musician who left us too soon, "Far out!"

On January 26, 2007, I saw a man, wife and daughter in prison. They had endured months of torture. The warden of the prison allowed them one day a week to shop, accompanied by a guard. The father made a choice to buy a small box of Q-tips and a pretty tin box.

The guards asked, "Why are you buying such simple and pretty things when you will soon die?"

"I want to enjoy and relish pretty things to make for me and my family. I then can carry a little beauty with me and not focus on the ugliness."

The guard mused. Then he set the man and his family free that very day. The man asked, "Why?"

The guard said, "I saw you buying simple things of beauty. It caused me to change and gave me hope. So I set you free."

When I awoke, I could feel tears in my eyes. Free! Now you become each person in the story. You can be the guard setting others free. You can be the prisoner and set yourself free! We have the keys to freedom from our prisons if we aren't afraid to use them.

I was reading about limiting beliefs and how they stop us. I watched a movie on TV called "Ransom." When the movie ended, it was almost midnight. I fell asleep again.

A maniac kidnapped my grandson. In order for me to ransom him, the kidnapper told me I had to tap dance! The maniac sent me a video of a master tap dancer. I was instructed to practice until I could perform at a master's level. I did so out of fear and anger at the maniac.

He then taped my performance and sent it to a "rebel" TV group. They sent my tape to 150 channels. While I was dancing, I suddenly let go of fear and anger and entered a calm altered state, like a Sufi Dancer. I went through the pain until I had a second wind of ecstasy.

In my waking time, I avoided excessive exercise. I was losing weight in order to slow down aging.

I danced like a child. I lost my inhibitions and false beliefs, one of which had been that I cannot dance! In the altered state, I was joyful. The euphoria in my mind and body went past all limits. It was incredible! Then I awoke.

As I was writing this down, I asked, "What are the beliefs that stop me physically, mentally, and spiritually? What is my fear and anger? Can they motivate me?"

I chose to stop being physically lazy about experiencing movement. I said, "Drop resistance! Take action. Ask what will happen if I don't. Conversely, what will happen if I do?"

I asked for joy, I dropped sadness, and I transformed to gladness. Dance like no one is watching! Guess what? The maniac was a Master teacher sent to me for fun, joy, and love! I gladly follow the teachings.

I realized through my dreams that I was adjusting to my new limitations and learning to accept who I was and what I was still capable of doing with my life.

Chapter 12
KEY II SAYINGS, QUOTATIONS, AND MEDITATION

To Muse!

Psalm 39:2 – "While I was musing, the fire burned."

Psalm 143:5 –"I muse on the work of thy hands. Man is only a puff of wind!"

Slowly the words came to my conscious mind. I knew I was a mystic and had been all of my life. I was working from within to awareness that this is my job. I decided to be an explorer and discover the uncharted parts of myself as well as I can and to my enjoyment.

It would create energy to do my work with others. My work to serve was not just a story but also a destiny. I prayed and danced as if I were communicating with God. I knew I would experience true happiness because the work within flowed out. It seems that wisdom and spiritual light flowed into my thinking brain to give me a feeling of worthiness. I remain open to share with others the various ways I muse.

I experience neither strain nor effort. Coming from that place, I am at peace. I relax mentally. I gain perspective about problems as an opportunity to spend more time musing.

One of my mentors is Emmet Fox. He describes how to create positive change by knowing what God is and gaining power from that knowledge.

"God is Boundless Love...Infinite Intelligence... Unfathomable Wisdom... Unspeakable Beauty...the Soul of man. I am the image and likeness of God, and I have the power of the Word...That Word goes forth charged with the power of God."...Emmet Fox.

To begin this exercise, suggest to yourself that you will be meditating, reflecting, or musing. Focus on the fact that you are seeking peace, joy, love, prosperity, and health in your life with increased health and energy.

Now be still. Be quiet. Relax. Search for your center of awareness that exists beyond your physical body, beyond any tiredness, any worry, and any pain. See what comes to your mind without editing your thoughts. Then ask your muse to open your entire being to spiritual guidance. Then again, be very still. Let your inner self be your guide on your quest. When you are at peace within yourself, look further inward. Find the part within that is in harmony with the universe. Keep your focus on seeking peace, joy, love, prosperity, and health in your life. Remain quiet for at least ten minutes. Practice often.

Write down your experience and put it away for about a week to ten days. Then read it again. Notice what you see. You are the seer. Go back now and read Psalm 39:3, "While I mused." Jesus in Matthew 6:22—"The lamp of the body is the eye." Keep that thought in your mind. What is it you see? What do you perceive?

Jesus goes on to say, "Let your eye be sound and to be sound is to be whole and healthy, morally healthy!" Then he says, "Your whole body will be filled with light!" Will you see?

Self-hypnosis is a form of meditation. Learn self-hypnosis from a book or qualified teacher. What I do: Choose an object like a flower, rock or a lighted candle. Fix your eyes on the object. Be comfortable. As you stare, take 3 or 4 deep breaths. Count to five and exhale. Suggest something like the following in your own words: "As I breathe gently and stare at the object, my eyelids will grow heavier." Soon you will close your eyes. Repeat. Continue to relax. Now repeat, "I am relaxing deeply now." Repeat with eyes closed 3 to 5 times.

With every breath, you will go deeper and deeper into hypnosis. Then you must relax your whole body, part by part. Start with your feet, repeating the word, "relax," then your right leg, then the left leg. Let all muscles be limp and loose and heavy. Repeat for each body part:

hips, stomach, chest, neck, and shoulders. Repeat that they are heavy and warm.

Now let your back and chest relax, letting the body feel warm and heavy. Continue this phrase, "Heavy and warm," for shoulder, neck, head, and suggesting that you are going deeper and deeper into self-hypnosis. Slowly keep repeating the words as you visualize walking down a gentle slope. Then continue to breathe softly as you enter the hypnotic state.

I chose as my symbol the butterfly. As you know, symbols reveal the inward

mind. Thus the chrysalis represented for me the time of being in a cocoon of my own making. When the time was right, I came out of that into the new me. It was a shift from "that" to now. My intuitive part—a sixth sense—opened my soul through the spirit within to complete my karma. Then I could restore my inner sprit to a new level: physically, intellectually, emotionally, sexually, and be the social me.

I chose the butterfly spontaneously to open up deep respect for myself to be at one with nature. My grandmother was a Native American, probably of the Algonquin tribe. Being one with nature became my central core for spiritual life. The Navajo nation describes health as "walking in balance."

I chose many models of persons who personified deep wisdom. I found quotes by those considered wise and who have manifested that wisdom into their lives.

Stop, take a breath, and exhale slowly. Now open your mind to the following quotes:

"Only the familiarity with the thoughts of death creates true inner freedom."—Albert Schweitzer

"I tell you solemnly, unless a wheat germ falls on the ground and dies, it remains only a single grain; but if it dies, it yields a rich harvest."—St. John 12:24

"Whom do you fear? Who can you kill? Soul is not born, nor does it die."—Bhogavard Gita

Now repeat the above quotes over slowly. Breathe in and out. Now, muse.

If I see I am fully present, I am in the Now. The Psalm says that while I was musing, the fire burned! The price is that we will pass through the fire. If we love like a red-hot flame, we will also suffer. We suffer to burn off the gross. As we go through loving and suffering, we find we are on the Jesus Path. See? Learn through metaphors in order to go further into truths, such as "There is not a nowhere, because God is everywhere."

A childhood prayer: "God is great. God is good." Therefore, God is love and loves you. Then take a quantum leap. "Love one another and ourselves exactly as God loves us."—Ephesians 5:1. Breathe in the essence of what you see.

What is interesting to me is that every time I muse like this, I am never quite the same as I was before! Each musing results in my inner growth! Note I Corinthians 2:13—"We teach spiritual things spiritually!" Contemplate love. Now, love another like God loves you. Figure it out!

As I mused, I learned to live with paradox—contradictions and balanced opposites. Here I want to introduce an experience I had in Athens, Greece, at the Parthenon. As I stood looking out toward the hills, I had an urge to write or draw something that represented balance and wholeness. The essence was wisdom, or Sophia, the Greek goddess of wisdom.

What the caterpillar calls the end of the world, the master calls a butterfly—Richard Bach, Illusions.

There is a Perfect Concept of Man, held in the Mind of the Universe as an already accomplished fact, but man is subject to the law of his own choice.—The Science of Mind.

To me, the butterfly represents the gift that comes out of every seeming tragedy, as in Richard Bach's statement above. Sometimes the butterfly emerges immediately, but other times it takes a much longer time to emerge from the cocoon. Some gifts come to assist the multitudes and some only for the one person experiencing the loss. But every seeming tragedy has a gift, such as the butterfly's beauty, when we step back for a clearer view or give the bigger picture time to emerge.

In truth, each morning is a rebirth, for each night we die to the old and awaken to be new. We cannot change yesterday, and we can only live to the highest and best right now. So each new day is a new canvas—a clean, clear slate—with nothing on it but what we imagine and make up in the moment. God gave us the mental capacity to make choices; each choice creates our life step by step. Choice by choice, every thought we think, every word we speak, and every action we take becomes our life. If we don't like it, we can choose again new thoughts, new ideas, new words, and new actions, getting new and different results. It is up to each of us to stand guard at the portals of our minds to watch our thoughts. We have unlimited potential. Each one of us is made in the image and likeness of God, with all the qualities of the Master. We have the choice of how we use the gifts and talents that have been given to us.

Affirmation

I know that within every experience is a gift for me. I know that I am at choice in every moment of my life; I choose joy, love, happiness and peace. I express my talents and gifts to the benefit of the world. —Audrey Turner, July 8, 2002

Live in the sunshine, swim the sea, and drink the wild air. —Ralph Waldo Emerson

Thousands of tired, nerve-shaken, over-civilized people are beginning to find out that going to the mountain is going home, that wilderness is necessity; that mountain parks and reservations are useful not only as fountains of timber and irrigating rivers, but as fountains of life —John Muir

Time is too slow for those who wait, too swift for those who fear, too long for those who grieve, too short for those who rejoice, but for those who love, time is eternity. —Henry Van Dyke

Sometimes your joy is the source of your smile; but sometimes your smile can be the source of your joy. —Thich Nhat Hahn

The wilderness and the idea of wilderness is one of the permanent homes of the human spirit. —Joseph Wood Krutch

Alphabet

Another way of meditating is to choose a letter of the alphabet and make a list of words starting with that letter. Then take each word and close your eyes for 1 or 2 seconds and repeat it. Now go on to the next word and repeat. When you have completed the list, go back asking which word stands out at this moment. Write that word down and read it over several times until you sense its meaning for you.

Now ruminate on how you can carry out this word and what it means to you. Take a breath, close your eyes and imagine adding that concept to your behavior. Ready? Get set! Go!

Begin with a list of A's

Actualize

Affectionate

Active

Affinity

Analyst

Astute

Attitude

Autonomous

Awe

Azure

Affluent

Association

Accommodating

Next list your B's

Being

Bless

Beatitude

Be gentle

Beloved

Breathe

Bliss

Biological

Beneficence

Benevolence

Benediction

Believe

Beliefs (of others like Jesus, Buddha, etc.)

I did choose to follow my mystical path by expanding my beliefs. I encourage you, too, to read from many books on spirituality. You could start with Jesus and Buddha.

Now the C's

Change (belief and behavior)

Completeness

Commitment

Coping

Clarify

Cognitive reframing

Cognitive distortions

Contemplation

Consider options

Creative breathing in alpha state

Counsel

Create soul mate

Compassionate

Charitable

Connection to cosmic wisdom and intelligence

Consequences

Create inner peace

Counseling in compassionate and charitable state

I

Intuition

Imagination

Illumination

Inspiration...inspire, breathe...more intellect and emotions... prompt action

Intelligent

Intellect

Inner...intra psychic

Icon...likeness...image

Ideals

Identity

Imagery

Impressive

Improve

Incarnate (actualize)

Incite (stimulate—put into action)

Income

Increase

Infinite

Influence

Instruct

Integrate

Intention

Inter weave

Intimacy

Invent

-ize...cause to be or become

L

Letting go

Life

Light

Love

Laughter

Lightness

Learner

Lever

Lean

Liberty

Logos

Loyal

Lucent

Luck

Luxuriant

Lusty

Leave

Lyrical

Lucid

Large mindedness

Longing for

Levity

M

Meaning

Magnificence

Matching

Magnetizing

Money

Moderation

More

Material

Mutual friends

Mutual companions

Mystic

Metaphor

Musing

Mastery

R

Reprogram

Reframe

Reliable

Recline

Reenergize

Reward

Reason

Rehearsal

Reaffirming

Results

Relate

Reap

S

Serve

Soul...starlight...radiant...star...sublime

Seven

Synchronicity...time...space...inner connected...one

Synthesis

Synergy

Spirit...energy...Ruach Elohim...Holy Spirit

Still

Solid...grounded

Simultaneously...past...present...future...now

Seer...see here and there, over there...relativity

Sage...solver...solution

Seeds...thoughts...seed: sow for future

Space...inner and outer...time continuum...renew:
shape shifter

Shamanistic

Sequential...patterns...cause and effect

Simplicity

Symbolic

Study: create life situations

Strength...steadiness...stand

Stories

Saver

Spiritual wisdom...inner light...self-regeneration

Serene

Success...reward

Sinuous...sensing

Speak up and out...self-expression

Slender...slim...stretch...supple

Sing

Smile

Seeker...stimulation...scintillating

Stable...serious...sensible

Strut your stuff! Stay on track!

Sunny...optimistic

Serenity

Serendipitous

Self-knowledge...confidence...integrity

Study/student of

Sharing...supporter

Strive

Systematic

Sympathetic...sensitivity

Suggest to inner mind—

Stop stopping self!

Smile...sing

Stretch: Qi Gong...Tai Chi...massage...walk...stride

Start: moving body...dance...drum...taking action on what you want to do

Show: feelings

Solve...stop...grinding teeth...psychogenic

Subconscious: ask, suggest and dream

Speak out and up

Stop...Procrastination! Sitting so much!

Serve...seek help...spending time...how?

Study...skills...enhance your knowledge...spending time

Sharpen

Silence...Zen, do

Satisfaction...satisfy

Save

Share

Stimulate

Stressors...self-denial patterns that slow down joy and happiness

Strokes: self and others

Sleep

W

Wonderful...wise...wizard...within

Wag

Waken

Water

Wealth

Wean

Weep

What is...who says so?

Will

Win

Wind

Wisdom

Wise Wit

Work

Worth

Write

Wrong

Wrought

Why?

Poetry

To paraphrase from Lewis Carroll's *Alice in Wonderland*—

When you turn into a chrysalis, you will someday you know,

And then into a butterfly,
Don't you think you'll feel a little queer?
The Caterpillar answered "Not a bit."

Chapter 13
KEY III SYNERGISM, SYNCHRONISM, AND POETRY

Here are some of the short poems I wrote over the years that came about as the result of my musing. I encourage you to keep a journal and do the same.

The Butterfly

I drove into the hills while musing.
I sat with my window open
Listening to the sound of birds.
Bees were humming from flower to flower.
A butterfly flew in and landed on my finger. Its feet held
onto me,
Touching me. I touched it. It became me. I became it.
For those brief moments I shared love, and life, and
beauty.
Then it flew away.
Butterflies are free.

The Enchanted Swan

The flag ruffed in the gentle wind.
Colors flashed like a sunbeam.
The breeze stopped.
The colors died.

Love is the wind.
We are the flags.
An enchanted swan
Floated to the enchantress.
She uncurled her graceful
Neck in unison with his.
Their bills touched,
Caressing.

The Empty Shell

Yesterday, an empty shell
Washed up on the shore,
An empty thing.
A sea snail carved his shell,
Now his empty shell,
Lying next to hers
On the sand,
An empty thing.

Disappointment

The Hummingbird returned.
The sweetness of the fuchsia
Had called him back.
But only cold winds greeted him.
He hoped for more, but found
Only moisture on a new bud.
He tasted but
Flew away again.

The White Water Lily

The white water lily
Floating serenely upon
The mirrored pool
Quietly.
A Spirit of Calm.
A Time of Peace.

The Dead are Gone

All the dead are gone.
The earth spins on through space.
We nod as they pass.
Then we search for
What's next?

Waiting

Cruel winds chill the heart.
The spirit waits
Knowing that spring will come again.

Knowing Sorrow

He who has not
Looked on sorrow,
Will never know
Day.

Love and Loss

I saw the gentle mist.
It sprinkled the world.
I saw love.
I was made new...
Again.
For a brief moment

Starlight

A star flared brightly.
Then like love,
Its light slowly died.

Loving

In all beginnings
Dwells a magic force
For guarding us and
Helping us to live.
In the light of everything,
Live now
As long as you can.
And Love as long as you live.

Lost Love by Michael Petrillo
Lost in a masquerade,
Tried to talk.
The words got in the way.
If you can't meet me

Inside,
I'll meet you somewhere
In between.
Every time we go forward,
We leave something
Of ourselves behind.

Empty Shells by Michael Petrillo
For my own amusement,
I gathered shells
By the shore
Once inhabited, now empty.
Like the hollow words of lost love
Only emptiness.

Observations by Michael Petrillo
The words do not tell us how to feel.
As a short observation, they
Are cosmic linked poems.
Look, hear, touch, taste, and
Share the experience and perceptions
With others. Observe.

Observations II by Michael Petrillo
A client wrote
You have counseled me
With stop watch in hand.
I was aware of your hand.

Thorns by Michael Petrillo
Music stopped when she left.
Song behind impaled by
Thorns of grief.
And the butterfly died.
Dragonfly thought he was safe
Flitting on shiny wings.
Frog's sticky tongue
Flicked out.
Life is not safe.
Somewhere over the light
There is a silken web
In space.
The spider spinning
Web of beauty and loss.
As I mused, I saw a butterfly, a symbol of my inner self.

Take Flight

A delicate butterfly
Is love.
It matters not there are
Many species.
Fly.

Song of Love

Waves reaching to the sky
Falling, crashing into the ocean.
Roaring to the shore

Whispering to the sand.
Tears welling up in eyes,
Spilling over, running
Down face.
Soon dried up.
I found a seashell.
It had a song inside.
I gave it to you.
Now both of us
Still have the song.

Haiku

Read about haiku, a form of poetry. A very good book to read is The Haiku Handbook by William Higginson with Penny Harter. Cost is about $15.00.

I had a wonderful, witty friend in Livermore. With two others, we had breakfast each week. We covered the gamut of subjects. One morning, he brought in Haiku poetry. He had been invited to Japan to present his works to a world conference on Haiku poetry.

I asked him to teach me to write Haiku because it appealed to me the minute I read Gerald's works, especially his book on cats! He taught me the formula and encouraged me to write and to meditate about nature.

The form of Haiku is simple: 5 - 7 - 5. It's a short poem of 3 lines. A Haiku of 5 lines would be 5 - 7 - 5 - 7 - 7. Traditional

Haiku portrays nature, creation, and creatures. It was written as an art form and for amusement. The original style has been expanded, but much is based on the following measures. It has seventeen syllables in 3 lines, though one poem used 31 syllables: 5 - 7 - 5 - 7 - 7. Also: 7 - 7 - 5 - 8 - 7 - 5 and 5 - 7 - 5 - 11 - 7 - 7.

A few examples of Haiku follow:

> Don't worry spiders.
> I keep house
> Casually.

> The butterfly,
> Dressed in gold,
> Off to the garden.

> A moth darts
> In moonlight
> Above the lilacs.

I am an amateur! However, I wrote, sometimes correctly, other times not correctly. Please look past the form. But do begin your own collection of Haiku poems. Focus on nature, on beauty, and on what you love. Begin by quietly musing, and then write.

The Next Stage-Utilize Synergism and Synchronism

I wrote to extend my musing. I chose to express what was the result of meditation and a desire to share my innermost thoughts. I hope you get the bug! One idea that helped me was that I was doing it right for me. The right reading, meditation, and synergism will work together to improve my work. Now it is your turn. Open up to the synergism you need to grow to the next stage.

"Whatever you vividly imagine, ardently desire, sincerely believe, and enthusiastically act upon...must inevitably come to pass!"

— Paul J Meyer, Author

Just a bit of history to see how I integrated my life, revised some paradigms, and made a series of steps to become a new recognized entity.

I am the founder and Director of the Inter-Faith Counseling Service, Inc. We are an organization to "provide spiritual, psychological, and mental health service to the areas of Alameda, Contra Costa, San Mateo, and Monterey Counties, California, as of February 4, 2000."

As my spiritual side evolved, I, as a product of intense meditation, was guided to take a step to form a group based on my intuition and wisdom.

Thus came into existence the founding of The Order of Melchizedek.

Chapter 14

KEY IV   SPIRITUAL WISDOM
AND INNER LIGHT

The Founding of The Order of Melchizedek

The words "God is Love" present a paradigm that underlies mystery, metaphysics, and mysticism and is expressed by spirituality. It is based on the sacredness of life.

Melchizedek was the Priest-King of Jerusalem and peace. He prepared and served a ritual meal to Abraham, who gave a title to Melchizedek. (Genesis 14:18-20)

Melchizedek represents and is a mythical figure that existed before the Old and New Testaments. He is symbolic of mystery, mysticism, and metaphorical spirituality, all of which existed before written sacred literature into which we can also tap. He stands for all those who are called to serve. He mystically reveals the meaning and purpose of life beyond religion and transcends man's efforts to put faith in a limited box of conformity or a single creed or "ism."

The unknown writer of the New Testament book of Hebrews (Hebrews 7:1-28) reveals metaphorically Christ

as the High Priest after the order of Melchizedek. Christ is the Cosmic Light.

I have revealed profound experiences here that I have never written down before. These experiences, as well as my years of study, have led me to express these thoughts that previously I have shared with but a few wise persons. They all indicated with gratitude that I stated something that was simmering on their minds. It helped them realize they, too, were called to serve.

Why now? It is time to pay my tithe by publicly revealing what I have been practicing.

You are invited to become a member of the Sacred Order of Servers.

It was very rewarding to work with people who were attracted to the idea of serving; hence we call ourselves "The Sacred Order of Servers."

I made a decision to legitimize our informal group. This we did on August 11, 2006. I did not know that events would transpire that I was not ready for, but they freed me from the past to concentrate my energies.

Three major events took place. First, I had a dream that I was going to experience another change in my life.

Second, I was diagnosed with Peripheral Neuropathy. It forced me to give up driving and close my counseling practice office as an L.M.F.T. and psychotherapist.

Third, I discovered that, through counseling with a very knowledgeable minister, I could practice counseling under the Business and Professional Code of California. It states that as an ordained minister I could practice as a pastoral counselor!

As I mused, I experienced inspiration and a sense of new purpose for my life. I might add that I was 84 on my birthday on January 7, 2011, and I still am excited about life.

In addition to that, for several years I had been writing thank you notes to people I heard about who were giving their time and energy to helping others.

Actually, when I tracked down my correspondence, one of the first letters I wrote was to Dag Hammarskjold, a man of peace. Tragically, he died soon after in a plane crash.

I also wrote a letter to Mother Theresa. She replied in a most gracious personal note. It ended in asking me for a donation to her Leper Project! We all like to be appreciated and have someone say thank you.

The following is from readings on destiny and meditation from the Brihadaranyaka Upanishad IV, 4.5

You are what your deep, driving desire is.
As your desire is, so is your will.
As your will is, so is your deed.
As your deed is, so is your destiny.
The Laws:
Pure Potential—Be. Be still...30-30 and non-judgmental.
Karma: Cause and effect
Least effort
Intention and desire
Detachment
Dharma—Purpose in life
The Journey—To see the Divinity within us.
The Law—As you process, the manifest becomes the Divinity.
Transforming—Observer becomes the observed. Seer becomes the seeker.
Spirit—Divinity in motion; object of creation of the physical and consciousness.

From Goethe, 1771

"When paradigms change, the world itself changes with them."

How am I seeing the world? Choose to see the world in new ways, and then change the world that is there for us to see.

Often we are so constituted that we believe the most incredible things. Once they become engraved upon our memory, woe to him who would endeavor to erase those beliefs.

You can create your own reality, you know. There is no better time to try than now.

During a time as I mused, the psychic part of me saw me as a priest, shaman, and healer. The image that came to mind was a diagram I drew in Athens, Greece, at the site of the Pantheon. It was luminous and the lines were energy connections. I labeled it The Christ Principle.

Through thought processes, I envisioned the Infinite channeling through me: Love! Power! Intelligence! Wisdom! Wholeness! The energy, like a step-up transformer, gave me a strong desire to express love, power, hope, health, and success in doing spiritual service as a healing, loving man.

I made a list using the word Be—

Nice
Friendly
Strong
Wise
Healthy
Wealthy
Giver
Receiver
Mindful

Kind

Loving

Healer

Serene

Patient

Peaceful

Spiritual—High emotional quotient

"People are like stained-glass windows. They sparkle and shine when the sun is out; but when the darkness sets in, their true beauty is revealed only if there is a light from within."

—Elisabeth Kubler-Ross

Illumination will come as man realizes his Unity with the Whole. Man constantly works to let Truth operate through him.

—Paraphrased from *The Science of Mind*

Light, An Ancient Symbol

The holiday season has many symbols. Of all the symbols, light is probably the most universally recognized. It isn't really known when the celebration of the Winter Solstice began. Whenever we did begin to recognize the Winter Solstice, light has always been a major part of its importance to us. From the lights that decorate stores, shopping malls, trees and candelabras, light has come to symbolize much of the festive spirit of the holidays.

As much as we enjoy this custom today, try to imagine what it must have been like barely one hundred-fifty years ago before the invention of the light bulb when the only available light after sunset came from fireplaces and candles. The many lights and candles at Christmas must have evoked gasps of wonder and delight. They were marvelous to us then, and they remain marvelous to us today. Was it just the outward light that was appealing after months of winter? We might ask ourselves what symbol did Light represent in our beliefs, both in ancient times and today?

Our ancestors understood that the longer days that begin with the winter solstice symbolize a growing inner light. They recognized that the short, dark days brought a time of rest for Nature. They lifted their spirits and organized their festivities and rituals around this time. Our current celebrations, such as Hanukkah and Christmas, continue with the light theme, but we often consider the symbolism and how it relates to external light rather than to inner wisdom.

The real illumination of this season shines from within each of us and is an enlightenment we experience from new realizations and insights. We must remember to open ourselves up and allow the light to enter. We must allow it to infuse our minds, our spirits, and our hearts. The light of spiritual wisdom can be realized within us when we take the time to become aware of it. We are sometimes challenged during the holidays to find time to do this, but we are rewarded enormously when we do.

My life's journey is cause for rejoicing. God's wisdom flows into my life and through me at every moment.

As part of my reading spiritual literature, I read The Sufi Book of Life. I have paraphrased a page that struck a chord in my mind.

The Sufi Book of Life

There is a way of looking upon the earth; rather than perceiving it through the senses, one contemplates a precognitive image that is inherent in one's soul. The scene of earth will trigger this image, which lies latent within. One's mind belongs to the sphere of Hurkalya, the sphere where creative imagination molds the archetypes of those forms that are eventually projected as objects, bodies of planets, or galaxies.

The light within us resembles the light of the farthest stars and galaxies, which are closest to the beginning of the cosmos. The Sufis meditated on this radiance in all being to inspire them to look behind the appearances of things. The following meditation is a part of this verse.

Light upon light upon light—back and back we trace it to its Source. Radiating light and sound—a voice, an echo guiding those who hear Love's desire, unfolds the universe's story.

Who comes to this call like thirsty birds to water?

Beloved, the One, creates for us models, signs, symbols, and parables; everywhere we look to remind us of our Source.

And the One behind all understands and embraces all—

the past and future journey of every thing from seed to star.

Perhaps life is calling you to take some time to reflect upon your life so far. What guidance have you received? What have you learned? What would illuminate your life's path further? Take some time to contemplate the job description of a human being, according to the Sufis; to reflect the divine image and express the consciousness and heart feeling of the entire natural cosmos that was created before humanity.

Roots and Branches

The traditional translation of this quality is "the light." The roots of Nur point to the constant new (N) and transformational (U) radiance of life (R). It derives from the same root as the Hebrew aor, the primal light created in the beginning, as described in Genesis. This light illuminates in a focused beam, like beacon lighting up a path. Nur also points to the archetype of the primal human being called Adam Qadmon in Jewish mysticism and Nur-i-Muhammad in Sufism.

Center yourself again in the heart. Breathe the name Ya Noor and follow the feeling of the sound deep into your heart of hearts. Find the whole world within your heart, and your heart within the heart of the One Being. Allow the light to enter your spirit and lighten your heart.

Chapter 15
KEY V WISE WIZARD WITHIN

Karen Armstrong in *The Science of Mind* spoke of the world's religions. "Religion comes to our broken world. We need to go in search of lost heart, the spirit of compassion that lies at the core of all our traditions."

Armstrong also tells us, "If we were to examine the basic principle of the religions of the world, we would find a great similarity among them."

A prayer for guidance. It is good to use it often, so know it well—

Today I begin a new life.
I will greet this day with love in my heart.
I will persist until I succeed.
I am nature's greatest miracle.
I will live this day as if it is my last.
Today I will be master of my emotions.
I will laugh at the world.
Today I will multiply my value a hundred fold.
I will act now.
I will pray for guidance.

When you learn it yourself, go out and take somebody by the hand and help him or her. Each must tread the path alone, but we can make a chain by linking hands and so lighten each other's way. As we begin to see and bring forth the good in each other, this becomes our reality.

> A voice asked,
> "Who is God?"
> The ocean roared, "I am."
> The tree softly swayed, "I am."
> A little newborn child cried, "I am."
> A yogi high in the Himalayan
> Caves chanted, "I am."
> Then a voice said,
> "Will the real God please stand up?"
> And the entire universe quietly stood up.

One morning as I was getting settled to meditate, I opened a book and inside was a letter from Mary Rose, who runs a shelter at the Covenant House for homeless children. Enclosed was a message from a nun to God!

"On the street I saw a small girl, cold and shivering in a thin dress, with little hope of a decent meal. I became angry and asked God: Why did you permit this? Why don't you do something about it? For a while God said nothing.

But that night, He replied quite suddenly:

I certainly did something about it—I made you.

Paths to Meditation

There are many ways to get started in meditation. Here is one to try. If you can, complete this in 20 minutes. If you don't finish, relax and do as much as you can. As you meditate, become aware of your own wise wizard within.

In a quiet place—

Sit very still with dignity and stability. Breath very gently feeling the breath run through your body. Let each breath bring calmness and relaxation.

Be aware of what feels tight within your body, mind, and heart. With each breath, feel a space open up to those closed-in feelings. Let your mind expand into an open space. Open your mind, emotions, and senses. Note whatever feelings, images, sensations, thoughts, and emotions come to you.

Each thought returns you to a connection with the Earth. Feel as if you were resting in the heart of your world. Appreciate these moments of stability and peace. Reflect on your emotions, feelings, and thoughts appear and disappear. Focus on your body. Feel the peace within your mind and spirit.

Sit this way for 10 minutes if you can.

Then slowly stand, take a few steps, and walk with the same inner awareness you felt when you were meditating. Be in contact with your inner wisdom, your muse. Write down your thoughts and your musings.

To learn more on meditation, refer to the following:

Meditation for Optimum Health, by Jon Kabat-Zinn and Dr. Andrew Weil (Sounds True: (800-333-9185): This two CD set is a first-timer's guide to the principles and practices of meditation.

The Relaxation Response," by Dr. Herbert Benson (Quill): The classic primer on the link between meditation and health. Not a guide on how to meditate.

The Meditation Year, by Jane Hope (Story Books): A beautifully rendered seasonal guide that describes various ways to meditate.

"The biggest myth is that as one learns to meditate, one will never feel upset. Meditation is not about getting rid of difficult experiences or feelings. It is about learning to cope with them."

—Cheryl Medicine Song Procaine,
meditation practitioner.

What's next? I found a system of psychosynthesis. Roberto Assagioli, M.D, founded it. It is a very well organized system that is client centered and provides the therapist with working models that can be taught to the client.

For some 60 years or so, Assagioli has been pointing to a particular experience of the self, which he believes is especially important in psychotherapy—and for that matter, in all of our efforts at growth. To Assagioli, the self is that center of consciousness that resides in each of us as the center of our being. It is the screen, the tablet, and the blank sheet upon which all of our experiences are projected. That is its receptive aspect. But it also has a directive function; namely, to initiate and guide our responses to the world about us. Within this system of psychotherapy exist these two ideas: (1) To expand our consciousness to enlarge the range of our awareness. (2) To increase our conscious control over our responses to the world. Basically, all therapy works toward these two goals. We might ask what is so different about psychosynthesis? Two things: (1) it makes these goals explicit from the start so they are in the forefront of our thinking; and (2) it offers specific techniques to help us accomplish them.

First, let us consider the definition of the expansion of consciousness. Corliss and Rabe (1969) in their book, *Psychotherapy from the Center*, describe the center of the psyche in terms that I believe Assagioli would readily accept as a good, phenomenological definition of the conscious, sentient aspect of the self. At the center, we are unaware of a purpose; and, therefore, without perceptual distortion.

To paraphrase from *Psychotherapy from the Center*, Corliss and Rabe (1969):

At our center, we are at rest, not from exhaustion but from our flexible balance. Our balance provides an instant reaction to change when necessary. No attachment must be broken for us to react elsewhere. When at our center, the quiet calm of simply being is an awareness of being available to one's self as need be.

Corliss and Rabe go on to state that to be at our center involves heightened sentience and awareness. These states are of a particular sort of action and are responsive, live states that exist and operate freely when self-preservation and ego problems are not at stake. When at our center, one acts in response to the demands of the situation, spontaneously, with no need for reward. When at our center, one has lost one's ego in our total attention and awareness. Therefore, the act of love is possible.

Centeredness is the state of being identified with one's self. When one is centered, one knows that we are all brothers and sisters under the skin; but one does so without losing one's sense of personal identity. As

Corliss and Rabe put it, we experience a disinterested impersonal empathy for the other, but we are not drawn into a sense of total identification with the other. We are still two distinct beings, with the polarity and exchange that is only possible when there is such differentiation. Differences are bridged by each person's sense of shared humanness.

Following is a brief summary of psychologist Frank Haronian's writings on intuition:

The intuitive function, which operates when thinking, feeling, and perception are suppressed, is a way of apprehending the totality of a given situation. At the same time, the insights gained from intuitive seeing must be checked against hard facts before they are to be accepted.

From the statement above, we realize that intuition can be seen as fleeting hypotheses. They sometimes arise spontaneously, but if we follow a simple procedure, we can find access to them. Often it is useful to have a particular problem in mind, applying every conscious effort to find an answer to the problem.

Next, we put aside the problem and relax physically. Follow the previous suggestions of entering a musing state. As our bodies relax, our emotions also tend to become calm. We muse. Finally, we turn away from the flow of images and ideas that habitually come through our minds, repeat the problem that is bothering us, and peacefully wait for an intuition that is relevant to the problem. Intuitions are fleeting and often obscure; they can be sometimes be symbolic in character. It is, therefore, especially important to note in writing whatever comes to mind so that it will be available for subsequent critical scrutiny. Continue with writing in your journal, writing Haiku, writing your musings, and writing your dreams. Write freely now and refer back to reading what you have written at another time. Make no judgment about the value of the writing. It's your writing, your thoughts, your ideas and it's important.

Another very important exercise is this one in Disidentification.

Exercise in Disidentification

Purpose—People have a tendency to live exclusively outside themselves. This exercise, coupled with the exercise of self-identification that follows it, affords a means of entering into oneself. First, we must disidentify from all that we are not. We must distinguish the inner self from our consciousness, from our emotions, our desires, our thoughts, our actions, and the roles we play. What we will find is that we are more than the sum of our behavior and experiences. We have a self, an essence that is not defined or limited by our outside self.

Procedure

As with all meditation, be comfortable. Be relaxed. Close your eyes, and breathe deeply. Look inward to achieve a calm state. Once you are in a state of calm relaxation, open your eyes and slowly read the following paragraphs.

My body is my way to experience the outer world, but I am more than my experiences in the outside world. I am more than my body.

I have emotions, I have feelings, but I can learn to direct and use my emotions. I am more than my emotions.

I have a mind that is active though not completely disciplined. I can learn. My mind is teachable. My mind brings me knowledge of the outside world, as well as my inner world. I can learn to direct and use my mind. I am more than my mind.

Now look inward and repeat the last line of each of the above paragraphs. Meditate about your inner being and how much more you are than what is ever known by the outside world.

Breathe and relax for an additional ten minutes.

Remember that we all have various activities many roles in life. These activities may at times express us, but they do not define our essential being. We may play at different times the role of wife or husband, parent or child, employer or employee, but we are something more than these roles. Our true nature is not identified with any outward role or activity.

Since we are conscious beings, here is the second exercise to check out your purpose and existential needs. The purpose of the exercise is to be used in conjunction with the exercise in disidentification. The exercise in disidentification should be gone through carefully first. After sufficient experience with the principle of disidentification, we can summarize its steps and proceed to self-identification.

What remains now that I have disassociated myself from my body, my feelings, my mind, and my actions? The essence of self, the center of pure self-consciousness, is what is left. It is that sense of being and of inner balance. This center of being affirms who we are and brings us its energy.

I will myself to achieve increasing meaning as well as direction to my life.

I will myself to detach from any emotion or thought from the point of an observer. I will myself to gain an understanding of the meaning of situations and their causes so that I may proceed to the most effective way to deal with my life.

This exercise is most effective if it is practiced daily. When possible, begin shortly after waking up and symbolically consider it a second awakening.

Modifications of the exercise can be done according to our own purposes by including other areas such as detaching from material possessions.

Ideas from *Meditation Notes: Writings of Ken Wilber*

I have desires, but I am not my desire. Desires are often changeable and contradictory. They are not myself.

My viewpoint is that there are various activities that play many roles in life. I must play these roles, whether it is the role of son or father, husband, wife, or friend. I know that I am more than the son, the husband, or the wife. These are my roles, which I play and which I can observe myself playing. Because I may step back and observe, I will find the most effective ways to deal with my life.

This exercise can be performed in groups. The leader states affirmations while members listen quietly, letting the words awaken the inner self.

Exercise in Self-Identification

Purpose
Having disidentified the "I" or self from the contents of consciousness (emotions, desires, thoughts) as well as from the body and outward behavior (roles, actions), one is prepared to see what emerges as a basis of self-identity.

Procedure
What am I then? Since I am able to stand back and observe my body, my emotions, my thoughts, and my actions, I must have a center of awareness that defines my essential nature. Just what is this center of awareness?

It is a center of pure consciousness and of will. It is the center that helps me realize that my body, my sensations, my feelings, my desires, my thoughts, and my actions are continuously changing from moment to moment from year to year. It gives me the sense of being, of continuity, of security. It is my source of identity.

I recognize my center of pure consciousness and of will. I realize it is capable of directing all the psychological processes and the physical body. It enables me to choose how I will respond to all inner and outer conditions. It enables me to initiate all activities.

I am the center and controller of both my consciousness and my will.

Chapter 16
KEY VI   EVOKING SERENITY

A Mystical Process

To speak more directly, and without metaphor, of the true relationship between intuition and intellect, intuition is the creative advance towards reality. Intellect has, first, the valuable and necessary function of interpreting; of translating, and of verbalizing in acceptable mental terms the results of the intuition. Second, intellect checks the validity of the interpretation; and third, it coordinates and includes intellect into the body of already accepted knowledge. These functions are the rightful activity of the intellect, without its trying to assume functions that are not its province. A really fine and harmonious interplay between the two can work perfectly in a successive rhythm between intuitional insights and interpretation; further insight and its interpretation; and so on.

The technique involved here is the use of the will to maintain the emotions in a quiet, tranquil state to evoke serenity. One of the favorable conditions toward the reception of intuition is when one is in a state of emotional quiet and not overly, emotionally involved. In achieving this, the Exercise in Disidentification that we dealt with earlier can be helpful. Also, the Exercise for Evoking Serenity given below is particularly applicable here.

Exercise for Evoking Serenity

1. Assume a physical attitude of serenity; relax all muscular and nervous tension; breathe slowly and rhythmically; express serenity on your face with a smile. (You can help yourself in this either by looking at yourself in a mirror or by visualizing yourself with that expression.)

2. Think about serenity; realize its value, its use, especially in our agitated modern life. Praise serenity in your mind; desire it.

3. Evoke serenity directly; try to feel it with the help of either the repetition of the word or by reading some appropriate sentence, or by repeating many times a suggestive phrase or motto. For example, you could repeat: "Both action and inaction may find room within; my body is agitated, but my mind is tranquil; my soul is limpid as a mountain lake."

4. Imagine yourself in circumstances that would tend to agitate or irritate you; for instance, being in the midst of an excited crowd...or in the presence of a hostile person... or confronted by a difficult problem...or obliged to do many things...or in danger. Now see, and feel yourself becoming calm and serene.

5. Pledge yourself to remain serene throughout the day no matter what happens; to be a living example of serenity; to radiate serenity. We respond to symbols. They have value. Intuitive understanding can often be induced by the use of symbols, which are subjective intuitive suggestions that are often illuminating. As subjects of meditation, they can be spiritual and have psychotherapeutic purpose.

One of my favorite psalms is Psalm 39.3, "While I was musing, the fire burned." It's a fire to kindle my imagination, gain insights, and develop meaning in life. Love is a symbol to open us to another person and for our communion with God. Open the soul to the light! Fire is a symbol, which opens the soul to spiritual awakening. Shakespeare expressed it, "Find tongues in these books, in running brooks, sermon in stones, and good in everything!"

Visualization on the Blossoming of a Rose

Let us imagine looking at a rose. Let us visualize its stem and leaves with a bud closed. It appears green because the sepals are closed, but at the very top a rose-colored point can be seen. Let us imagine this vividly, holding the image in the center of our consciousness. Now begins a slow movement as the sepals start to separate little by little, turning their points outward. As the sepals turn, they reveal the rose-hued petals, which are still closed. The petals also slowly separate . . . until a perfect, fully opened rose is seen.

At this stage let us try to smell the perfume of the rose, inhaling its characteristic well-known scent . . . so delicate, so sweet, so pleasant. Let us smell it with delight.

Identify with the rose. Symbolically, we are a flower, a rose. The miracle that animates the universe and created the rose is producing in us an even greater miracle—the awakening and development of our spiritual being radiating from us.

Through this exercise, we can effectively foster the inner flowering of our spirit and our connection with the universe.

Another form of musing taps into the wisdom of others. Over the years, I saved quotes, sayings, and written guides to create what I called my M.A.P.—Michael's Action Plan. The quotations were my mental and spiritual guides. After meditation I would tap into my deepest self to make concrete plans and take action.

How can we go about this? Read the sayings or quotes as if you were eating a mental meal. In the state of contemplation, allow your inner mind to digest the ideas and process them through your brain to create energy. Then channel the thoughts into reality and concrete action.

Read over the material several times a day, set it aside, and then read it again. Just before going to sleep, review the material. I have followed that pattern and mused before going to sleep for many years. My dream self would weave the thoughts into workable and logical thoughts. My inner muse would assert itself to heal wounds, solve problems, and present my next action plan.

Sometimes it would take days for answers to come. It is my hunch that my intuitive self was processing the thoughts, ideas, and plans before my brain said, "Go!" Inevitably, the answers came, but not in the exact manner I thought they would. I trust this process as a way to be wise and to carry out my plans. So far it has worked!

Here are some of the sayings, ideas, and instructions from my collection. The first is Albert Schweitzer's mantra that corresponds to my goals and desires.

"I don't know what your destiny will be, but one thing I know: the only ones among you who will be really happy are those who have sought and found how to serve."

Another great guide I have followed is Johann Wolfgang Von Goethe, a man of intellect, a scientist, and a mystic who stated the following:

"As soon as you trust yourself, you will know how to live."

Unless one sets his face in the right direction and makes a start, he will not reach his goals.

Goethe also said:

"Are you in earnest? Seize this very minute!
What you can do, or dream you can, begin it;
Boldness has genius, power, and magic in it.
Only engage and then the mind grows heated.
Begin, and then the work will be completed."

"Whatever you vividly imagine, ardently desire, sincerely believe, and enthusiastically act upon, must inevitably come to pass!"

When you actually learn to release the potential power of your mind, you will discover that it contains ideas of such creative value and wisdom that lack absolutely nothing!

Goethe again:
"What sort of God would He be who only pushed from without?"

"Let us seek to fathom those things that are fathomable and reserve those things which are unfathomable for reverence and quietude."

As long as you do not know
How to die and come to life again,
You are but a sorry traveler
On this dark earth." ...Johann Wolfgang Von Goethe

An echo of St. Paul, I Corinthians, 15.31... "I die daily."

The next quote has some key words that Goethe wrote characterizing his many accomplishments as writer, poet, musician, and more. He wrote poetry and stories that were put to music to become operas. Read carefully and then meditate on this next part that opens the mind to creativity and wisdom.

"Until one is committed, there is hesitancy, the chance to draw back, always ineffectiveness."

"Concerning acts of Intuition (and Creation), there is one elementary truth, the ignorance of which kills countless ideas and splendid plans—that the moment one definitely commits oneself, then providence moves, too."

All sorts of things occur to help one that would never otherwise have occurred once we commit to our inner wisdom and tap into the energy that is released.

"A whole stream of events issue from the decision, raising in one's favor all manner of unforeseen incidents, meetings, and material assistance that no person could have dreamt would come their way."

When all areas within are in sync, it is then that we find our spirituality and our wholeness. Our drive is naturally toward unity and equilibrium if we can learn to listen and to muse. Synergy is when it "all" works in unison. We are fully human then and blended into spirituality. My goal is to be fully alive and in tune with Nature.

Psalm 39:3 "While I was musing, the fire burned." Let ego melt, and use imagination!

BE: Crackle!
B – Believe I am spirit
C- Connect
R - Reality is manifesting all
A – Accept a matching connection
E – Energy...We are light!!
K - Kindness
L- Love

"Our doubts are traitors and make us lose the good we often might win by not fearing to attempt."
—William Shakespeare in "Measure for Measure"

The fire is energy flowing into all our relationships in harmony with our destiny to belong.

Teilhard de Chardin abandoned the literal interpretation of the creation account in Genesis to a metaphoric interpretation. The Roman Catholic Church was displeased because the interpretation undermined the doctrine of Original Sin. They prohibited De Chardin's works from being published in his lifetime.

This quote from the book, *The Phenomena of Man,* helped shape my meditations:

"Someday, after mastering winds, waves, tides, and gravity, we shall harness the energy of love, and for the second time in the history of the world, man will have discovered fire."

—Teilhard de Chardin.

Let's decrease the time for us to reach the Omega Point, the union point with God. The metaphoric mind is in the right half of the brain. It is where our intuition, emotions, and creative consciousness dwell. It is the transcendent mind, or metaphysical mind. It is the holistic brain, the inventor, integrator, motivator, creator, the analyzer, the fantasizer, the imager, the player; it includes rationality, linearity, and logic. It draws pictures and loves nature! It is in sync with the left-brain intellect, rationality, and human emotions including sexuality.

By the time I read his book, I had evolved from a narrow literal viewpoint to a theological metaphoric interpretation of the Bible. I was influenced along these lines by reading books that emphasized a mystic guidance of the light. T. De Chardin's book, *The Phenomenon of Man*, was an account of the unfolding of the universe to a vision of the Omega Point in the future. He saw human kind evolving in the future to a Christo genesis, following the command: "Let there be light."

T. De Chardin also wrote *The Appearance of Man*, expanding our rational part that he calls the noosphere.

As I mused at this point, I realized that I needed a breather before I chose the next series of quotes. Before you read, stop, take a breather and let your imagination tell a story or parable about the quotes. It is not good to try to absorb too much at one time.

Reading *The Center of the Cyclone* by Dr. John Lilly became a means for me to transcend many beliefs that had been planted in my mind in the past. Basic to what I am implying is the power of belief and how our beliefs can limit us. Dr. Lilly's book is an excellent guide or map about how beliefs and disbeliefs can affect our future. Here is an excerpt compiled from *The Center of the Cyclone.*

"In the province of the mind, what one believes to be true either is true or becomes true within certain limits, to be found experientially and experimentally. These limits are beliefs to be transcended."

"Hidden from one's self is a covert set of beliefs that control one's thinking, one's actions, and one's feelings.

"To transcend one's limiting beliefs, one establishes an open-minded set of beliefs about the unknown.

"There are unknowns in my goals toward changing. There are unknowns in my means of changing. There are unknowns in my relations with others in changing. There are unknowns in my capacity for changing. There are unknowns in my orientation toward changing. There are unknowns in my assimilation of changes. There are unknowns in my needs for changing. There are unknowns in the form into which changing will put me. There are unknowns in the substance of the changes that I will undergo, in my substance after changing.

"My disbelief in all these unknowns is a limiting belief, preventing and transcending my limits.

"By allowing, there are no limits; no limits to thinking, no limits to feeling, no limits to movement.

"That which is not allowed is forbidden. That which is allowed, exists. In allowing no limits, there are no limits. That which is forbidden is not allowed. That which exists is allowed. To allow no limits, there are no limits. No limits allowed, no limits exist.

"In the province of the mind, what one believes to be true either is true or becomes true. In the province of the mind there are no limits.

The language of the subconscious is symbolic—be very aware of what you 'feed' your inner self."

Both visualization and affirmations are what Emmet Fox, an early Unity Church teacher, called the mental equivalent. He describes how to go about creating positive change—

"So the key to life is to build in the mental equivalents of what you want and to expunge the equivalent of what you do not want. How do you do it? You build in the mental equivalent by thinking quietly, constantly, and persistently of the kind of thing you want, and by thinking that has two qualities: clarity or definiteness, and interest.

Emmet Fox believed that in order to bring health, right activity, your true place, and inspiration into our lives, we must form a mental equivalent of what we want by thinking very clearly about it a great deal.

As I mused, I asked myself what beliefs are still stored in my past, smoldering like coals, but suppressing and limiting my thoughts? What beliefs are keeping me from serenity?

Now ask yourself this question. What is underneath, unseen, but causing me to procrastinate? Suddenly, a small flickering thought popped in my mind about a class on writing. We were to write spontaneous ideas. I wrote a song about nature and its beauty using metaphor. The young teacher asked me to stay after class to discuss the paper. She said, "You were too sensuous and vivid. You should be embarrassed to write like that." I sensed that she was enjoying seeing me flush and emotionally confused. I was too mortified to speak up. I stammered and asked her if I could rewrite the paper. She looked like a grinning cat at my embarrassment. She allowed me to rewrite the paper, implying that I be careful in the future.

I went to a senior friend of mine and shared with him what happened. He read the paper and smiled! I asked, "What?"

He replied, "You unknowingly hit a button. She sounds as if she suppresses all sensuality, so she rebuked you because she probably thinks all men have dirty minds! I'll help you rewrite the paper the way she wants it." He did and I thanked him.

I copied it and turned it in. It was a "blah" paper, but it was wordy. She liked it and gave me a good grade. However, the memory was painful, so I suppressed a part of me that in a strange way made me self-conscious around many women for a long time. I learned to put off anything that I "had to do."

My paper gave God the credit for creating a beautiful world for us to enjoy. However, out of my awareness, a seed of inhibition was sown. Somehow I developed writer's block for some time after that incident.

Past traumas, stored out of consciousness, have a way of inflicting all kinds of negativity. Some traumas develop destructive feelings that lead to rage. In order to become aware of the causes, meditate; bring to awareness the out-

of-sight thoughts that cause the pain and regret. Know
that it is time to let it go!

Chapter 17
KEY VII   SYNTHESIS,
INTUITION, AND MUSING

At the end of the day, all things, good and bad, come to an end!

We came to Monterey in 1998 and bought a beautiful home in Corral de Tierra. It was ideal for both of us. It was 2.7 acres surrounded by a scenic easement of 20 acres. No one could build in our backyard!

I had a successful and fulfilling counseling practice. My office on Garden Road was ideal for my clients and me.

Diane enjoyed nature and all things of beauty. She was able to pursue art, photography, and see her many friends.

Then lightening stuck! Coming home from work in 2008, a dog ran in front of my car. I tried to hit my brakes but my right foot and leg betrayed me. Under the stress, my leg refused to obey! I soon was heading straight into traffic. My instincts finally took over, and I swerved to the left bank, hitting the berm. My Jaguar flipped over on the right side and plowed down the hillside. I was strapped in by the safety belt and hanging in space on the left side of the car.

A man climbed up and knocked on the sunroof. I hit the button so he could see in and talk to me. I asked the man to call Diane to tell her what happened.

Meanwhile, traffic was backing up for several miles and highway patrolmen were surrounding the car.

A patrolman tapped on the left window and asked if I was bleeding. When he saw that I wasn't, he asked, "Have you been drinking?"

I replied, "No! In fact I don't drink at all!"

He smiled and said, "The ambulance is here and the paramedics will get you out." I was stressed out and aching all over, but I didn't think I had any broken bones. I was taken to Community Hospital of Monterey Peninsula, which I knew to be top-notch.

In the hospital emergency room, the doctor did a CAT scan and then told me that my neck wasn't broken. What a great relief!

After I told him what happened, he recommended that I see a neurologist. I will add that he was a great guy with a great sense of humor and a delightful fresh brogue. His humor and friendliness certainly helped make the whole frightening situation more bearable.

At the neurologist's office, after a thorough exam, Dr. Shen said, "Michael, you have peripheral neuropathy. You should not drive anymore."

I handed the car keys to Diane and said, "Doctor's orders!" I have not driven since. I have been in excellent treatment with Dr. Centurion in Carmel. I also go to physical therapy at Ryan Ranch where both of my therapists, Will and Kate, are excellent and very professional.

I relate the incident to point out that we cannot predict the unknown. It could have been an instant end to my life. Instead, I survived and knew that I must write and share with others my musing so that they may grow to become better survivors as well.

I had to sell my beautiful Jaguar, close my office, retire my counseling license, and move into a home office. All in one moment, my entire life changed.

I went through depression and faced an existential crisis. Diane, my loving wife, stepped in and supported me emotionally through my adjustment. Her life was completely changed as well. She no longer has the freedom that she once had.

I spent many hours meditating and re-evaluating my goals in life. Diane came first, and she was and is my best friend and supporter through crises. I reflected on how many people I counseled who had also gone through severe trauma and change only to have their spouses leave them.

I felt blessed that I had faith and spiritual guidance that I tapped into. Most of all, I am fortunate that Diane stood by my side and let me know how deep her love was for me as I went through the many drastic changes.

I reinvented my professional life. Since I was an ordained minister with the American Baptist Churches, I sought and was supported by our executive minister to counsel. I found that according to the California Business and Professional Code No. 2908, ordained ministers may practice counseling so long as they do not claim to be doing therapy.

Through research, I discovered the following opportunities still available. Since I am certified by the state and the national organization as a hypnotherapist, I could continue to include it as part of my credentials and use hypnosis with my clients.

Additionally, I am a member and certified Professional Personal Coach of the International Coach Federation as well as being the director and founder of the Interfaith Counseling Service and a Pastoral Counselor.

I am a life member of the Employee Assistance Program, United States of America. I counsel employees by referral from E.A.P.A.

Also, my children have been great and gave me love and comfort through the trial of my transition and reinventing my life.

Integrating all of the above lifted me out of a sense of loss and grief giving me the ability to plan my new life with hope. I now have recovered both mentally and spiritually. However, I will always have to cope with peripheral neuropathy.

I continue to have an office at home, conducting coaching via telephone and doing consultations. I connected with other pastoral counselors. They have been supportive and very helpful to me as I shifted gears to a new role.

Another side benefit is that since I don't travel to the office, I have more time to write! It was always a desire to someday write a book to express my inner self.

So here goes!

I want to share some things that I have done and some creative thinking that came to me as a result of meditation, contemplation, and following my lifelong practice of musing.

Psalm 39, "As I was musing," has been a part of my life since college. I did not share this with any of my college friends. As I listened to Dr. Bob Jones, I sensed that often when he was speaking, his whole manner shifted from preaching to a state of free-flowing, spiritual thought. His whole demeanor was quiet and mentally creative. I now realize that he was musing, and his inner fire was poetically and dramatically sharing a spiritual viewpoint.

Also, Dr. Bob was a well-known Shakespearean actor. BJU presented at least one play by Shakespeare every year with Dr. Bob as the main character. I was privileged in that he chose me to be his understudy, giving me the opportunity to read his part in the play Richard III to the other players while on one of his many speaking tours. Dr. Bob took time with me to walk through his part as he was on stage with the other actors.

When I was a senior in high school, I took a course in Shakespeare from a teacher who helped all of us learn to really appreciate them. All of it worked together to instill in me a deep love of Shakespeare that began when I was still a young man.

I had never had a birthday party growing up since our parents never had celebrations. I had a girlfriend, Betty, who organized a party for my 16th birthday. I was overwhelmed by the idea. I didn't know that Betty had taken up a collection to buy me a gift. When I opened the package, it was a one-volume collection of Shakespeare's plays! I was surprised and joyful. Betty knew I would love it! What a great gift! Two books I love: The Bible and the works of William Shakespeare.

I have contemplated and mused about psychology, though I have never felt pulled to focus on just one theory of psychology. Being Synergistic, I chose parts for me to follow and to integrate into my own thoughts and practice as a therapist.

Synergism also plays a role in my spiritual beliefs. I wrote my doctoral thesis on the concept of wholeness or holistic beliefs and practices for churches and ministers. My thesis was A Study of Holistic Counseling. At its center was a method of parish ministry as a doctoral dissertation.

The word holistic is that of viewing man not mechanically, but rather from a mystical viewpoint. Man is a unity of body, mind, and spirit. Therefore, we emphasize the whole person who is integrated and experienced in human-spiritual love in the here and now.

Transformation within ourselves begins when we decide to change. I chose to be an authentic, spiritual, wise, compassionate person. I will explain this key idea:

"Without the transcendent and the transpersonal, we get sick...or else hopeless and apathetic. We need something bigger than we are to be awed by and to commit ourselves to."...Abraham Maslow, *Toward a Psychology of Being.*

A college professor at Stanford University, Dr. Peter Koestenbaum, was teaching a course on clinical philosophy. It was the first course I took that wove together philosophy and religion. It opened the door for an in-depth philosophy of existence. He taught that many good people had a painful emptiness, hollowness, despair, and isolation. Then he focused on the answer, "Love yourself." We have the freedom to choose our destiny, and claim our freedom.

As the course progressed, I had a full realization that I am a mystic and had a transpersonal worldview. I was free to choose a fulfilling life from a mystical viewpoint and acknowledge the reality of death.

Shakespeare expressed himself masterfully on the subject of death when he wrote:

> Cowards die many times before their deaths,
> The valiant never taste of death but once.
> Of all the wonders that I yet have heard,
> It seems to me most strange that men should fear,
> Seeing that death, a necessary end,
> Will come when it will come.

Julius Caesar, Act II, scene ii

The poet Dylan Thomas wrote: "Do not go gentle into that good night; old age should burn and rave at the close of the day. Rage, rage against the dying of the light."

We realize that death teaches us that we are alone, but so is everyone! Therefore, we share a common bond after all!

I choose intimacy rather than loneliness. I know my life has meaning, joy, companionship, and worth.

I am a mystic. Basically, I experience mysticism as a deep state of enlightenment in union with the Divine. Wisdom earns us an insight into reality. I saw that I could grasp truth as well as use my intellect to reason. When I am in this spiritual state, I am happier, healthier, and grounded in holistic thoughts. I am clear and at peace with others and myself.

Mantra

I am in the Now!
I am a Seeker.
I am becoming an Enlightened Human Being.
I seek Knowledge and Truth.
I am receptive to new Ideas.
I am a Seeker in the Now.

From the Bible in John 8:32, we find: "You will know the truth and the truth will set you free!" Love it! Doesn't that make sense? Yes!

I am a muse. I express therapy as an art. I see through the eyes of the Divine and the realm of the Sacred. Serendipitously, I was a member of the International Society of Transactional Analysis. To me TA was a creative tool to bring about wholeness and healing of the psyche.

The Bible taught me that love was the greatest quality I could have.

I Corinthians 13:13 –"Faith, hope, and love, but the greatest of these is love!"

The goal was for me to be a compassionate therapist as well as maintaining a deep level of spiritual relationships. It would mean the best psychology through my mystical self, with sound transpersonal psychology.

I want here to thank Dr. Pete Kostenbaum, who helped me go through my transition creatively. If you haven't read it, I recommend his book, *The New Image of the Person*, the theory and practice of clinical psychology. I attended his class at the San Jose State University around 1981.

Karl Menninger phrased it thus, "Only in the presence of some kind of belief can there be a truly moving concern for mankind."

For this liberating truth, Freud searched not in the fields of the sciences, but in the tabooed land of the emotions. From Pandora's jar of man's mind, Freud found hope. All of the potential evils that lie within the mind of man including selfishness, hate, greed, bitterness, cruelty, and more, are in us, but not only those. Slowly pervasive and neutralizing, comes love, and then perhaps because of love comes faith and hope.

Love, faith, hope—in that order. The Greeks were wrong. Of course hope is real, and of course it is not evil. It is the enemy of evil, and it is goodness. It is our duty as healers to estimate probabilities and to discipline expectations. But leading away from probabilities, there are paths of possibility, toward which it is our duty to hold aloft a light. And the name of that light is Hope. From hope, we will reach spirituality and serenity.

As I muse as a therapist, I know that the light burns away the darkness of despair and depression. I believe that metaphor and mysticism are the total commitment to a deeply spiritual life. They are one more expression of integration of the anxiety of Nihilism. Our goal is creativity.

Karl Menninger wrote ***The Vital Balance***, a book that shapes my thinking very positively. I share here what he said about the most powerful words of the missionary and theologian the Apostle Paul.

"In what is perhaps the most beautiful short essay ever written by a theologian and missionary are listed the three great, permanent goods: Faith, Hope, and Love. Of these, Dr. Menninger declared, Love is the greatest."

Better acquainted with the sins and the suffering of mankind than most of his contemporaries, Saint Paul cried for all humans, "Wretched man that I am, who will deliver me from this body of death?" He did not refer here to physical death, but rather Saint Paul was describing the human situation, the dilemma of all people. For it he offered the famous social prescription implicit in his Corinthian essay.

Today, after twenty centuries, this prescription is taken very seriously in psychiatry. We would even go as far as to say that it describes the best philosophy of the psychiatrist. Faith, hope, and love are the three tangibles.

Love

Thousands since the time of Saint Paul have attested to the importance of love. Love is a great, selfless concern. We all want deeply to love and be loved. Love is stronger than hate. When we accept love with hope, the acceptance transforms us.

Dr. Peter Kostenbaum, expressed the concept of consciousness:

"Consciousness is a spiritual black hole. And that is the ultimate reality within your own soul. Can you feel the cold breezes of that nothingness?

"The key to the religious answers to life's eternal questions lies right at this point. You must understand the meaning of consciousness as transcendental."

Paraphrasing Dr. Kostenbaum, we can continue that line of thinking in the following way.

Metaphorically, God is supernatural. He exists outside the world much as the world of consciousness does. Both are regions waiting for exploration. They are visible only after learning the art of looking inward, stepping back, and moving away from the world. If we open our hearts to transcendental consciousness, we can make the exploration of inner consciousness a primary lifetime obligation and privilege.

The most beautiful thing we can experience is the mysterious. Some brain researchers have shown a mystical bent in some of their studies.

Charles Hendle, professor of philosophy at Yale, encouraged Penfield's book, *The Mystery of the Mind*. It was a much-needed encouragement, since the other neuroscientists to whom Penfield had shown his early draft discouraged him from proceeding with the project. To them, Penfield's speculative leap from neurophysiologist to philosopher was unscientific. At Hendle's urging, Penfield proceeded to detail, "how I came to take seriously, even to believe, that the consciousness of man, the mind, is something not to be reduced to brain mechanisms."

Why should it be surprising that the study of the human brain often leads to mysticism? Consider the paradox involved: The inquiring brain is itself the object of its own inquiry. The brain is the only organ in the known universe that seeks to understand itself. Looking at it from this point of view, we might expect a greater number of brain scientists to turn toward mysticism.

Along these same lines, Dr. Richard Restak, author of ***The Brain***, asks "After all, are not our brains part of the same physical universe whose essential nature remains, after years of research and speculation, essentially mysterious?"

As I mused, I wondered about joy. Can psychology bring joy? I recalled a book written by Scott Hamilton discussing what psychology actually is. The following is an excerpt from Scott Hamilton's book, ***An Introduction to Psychology.***

"Psychosophy is a new school of psychology emerging from a fusion of five foundations: psychology, philosophy, spirituality, growth, technology, and creative actualization."

In other words, it is a fresh psychological paradigm integrating new methods for viewing and understanding human nature, new ways of realizing philosophical truth, new approaches to deepening and exploring one's spiritual experiences, new techniques for joyous growth, and a new art of conscious creativity. Psychology empowers us to discover the truth based on direct experience of what actually works in the real world—both inner and outer. All aspects of psychology are open to change and to improving the quality of our own and other's lives. Such improvement is the sole purpose of psychology.

A new paradigm can unite five fields of psychology into a path meeting our human needs for understanding our own nature.

These five fields unite elements of the past school of psychology, including a new research methodology and new models of human nature, with research on development, relationships, creativity, consulting, and education. We can view psychology as the following:

- A new research method.
- The method looks experimentally at a verified model of human nature.
- The model presents new understanding of human development, and
- A new understanding of human relationships, and
- A new understanding of human creativity.
- All of these are integrated into new consulting and educational systems.

This sequence offers a vast array of powerful, profoundly effective resources to ever more fully contact and live from your innermost self. Psychology's working principles, models, and transformational techniques, free you to become self-nurturing and to enjoy self-discovery as well as self-expression. This inner growth steadily builds all your creative endeavors, from preparing and enjoying life-filled food, to building deep, loving relationships, to clarifying and actualizing your life's purpose.

In addition to being a new school of psychology, psychosophy is also offered as a new word. What does the word "psychosophy" mean? Since it points to a subjective experience, many definitions could be given. The inner definition, which must always stand above any others, is that psychosophy (from Psyche, meaning innermost essence, and Sophia, meaning loving wisdom) is living using the most wisdom of your innermost essence.

The Psychosophy School of psychology, with its five foundations and new models, assists you in joyously doing just that. It is a starting point for you to learn the real psychosophy within. Psychosophy is you, the self within, freely playing within your personal universe, creating and sharing with the great family of Being. Psychosophy is your innermost essence emanating its inner love and wisdom into your life.

Musing in Summary

I muse before I go to sleep. I make lists and notes, brief and to the point. Then I ask, "What's next?" I breathe softly and relax. I place my hand over my heart and breathe pleasant thoughts into my body. Then I ask my dream-self to answer my questions. I am serene as I fall asleep. I often wake up at night and go to my office. I then jot down ideas and answers to my questions from my dream-self before I return to sleep.

Dreams tap into our inner wisdom. Listen to your dreams as they open the door to the inner power of the unconscious. Ask yourself what are the symbols from our unconscious selves?

In *Man's Search for Himself* by Rollo May, we read about dreams. "(We)...understand our dreams, but we cannot understand ourselves!"

Dr. Erich Fromm's book, *The Forgotten Language*, teaches that dreams are in reality part of the one universal language shared by all mankind. Fromm's book is to be recommended to the nontechnical reader who wishes to relearn something about subconscious language.

Dr. Fromm's attitude toward dreams and expressions of the subconscious and unconscious aspects of ourselves was that dreams were expressions not only of conflicts and repressed desires, but also of previous knowledge that one has learned, possibly many years before, and thinks he has forgotten. The person who has become skillful in understanding what is being said in dreams can sometimes get from dreams valuable hints and insights into solutions to problems.

Rollo May believed that creativity exists in harnessing universality and making it flow through the eyes of the artist.

Think for a minute about intuition. What is it? Intuition is to have eyes that can look within to tap our innate abilities to create change.

Here's a Change Map of c's that came to mind during a time of meditation. It also reminded me to keep it simple.

Change Map

Community: Health, Wholeness, Safety, Healing, Self-disclosure.

Commitment: Abstinence, Group Consensus.

Coping with Cravings: Plan Interventions. Believe that urges will pass if you don't act on them.

Clarify Triggers: List the triggers. Be aware and avoid them.

Change Behaviors: List new behaviors. Work to change old behaviors.

Cognitive Reframing: Read Six-step reframe. Study steps to change.

Challenge Distortions and Pathological Beliefs: List and work to change them.

Contemplation: Become a seeker of knowledge. Be free from false beliefs. Expand your feelings of self worth.

Contemplate: Learn moderation in life behaviors.

Contemplate: Let spirituality become your drive towards wholeness. We have an internal healing blueprint through spirituality to wisdom!

Consider the Options: Know the options to drinking or to using drugs. Use the options to achieve wholeness and health.

Coping with Slippage Options: Know what to avoid. Call for comfort, support, and care from others in the group.

Completeness: Be fully human and be fully aware of the present. Work to achieve self-actualization.

Cosmic Wisdom: Faith, Hope, Love. Become connected to spirituality and intelligence.

Centeredness: Awareness of body and stressors.

Consequences of Immoderate Drinking or of Using: Behaviors. Consequences. Beliefs.

Creative Breathing: Into Alpha State

Intervention: Relaxation using One Home Mantra. The O H M, a spiritual practice that leads to inner peace and harmony. Let go of fears, anger, guilt, sadness, and negativity.

Exercise: Maintain a weekly regiment

Play: Sensual pleasures, humor, smile, laugh!

Autogenic Training

Self Hypnosis plus suggestions.

Counseling: Call for Telephone Therapy.

Plan to be compassionate and charitable.

Healing Symbols: Imagery, Visualizations.

Sleep: R.E.M.

Daily Mantra—I Am Present Now As a Healthy, Spiritual Human Being

In all areas, find balance and moderation in your life. Practice good nutrition by balancing insulin secretion.

Minimize refined sugars, fat intake, salt, and caffeine. Eat complex carbohydrates, fiber foods, less meat, substitute vegetable protein. Eat to enjoy, not to fill. Moderate alcohol. Consider trying a daily vitamin supplement.

"Whatever you can do or dream you can, begin it. Boldness has genius, power, and magic in it. Begin it now!" –Goethe

PSALM 39

To the chief Musician, even to

Je-du-thun, A Psalm of David.
I Said, I will take heed to my
Ways, that I sin not with my
Tongue: I will keep my mouth
With a bridle, while the wicked
Are before me.
I was dumb with silence, I
Held my peace, even from good,
And my sorrow was stirred.
My heart was hot within me,
While I was musing the fire
Burned: then spake I with my
Tongue.
Lord, make me to know mine
End, and the measure of my days
What it is; that I may know how
Frail I am.

Behold, thou hast made my
Days as a handbreadth; and
Mine age is as nothing before.

The result of David's musing came as an answer. He put a new song in my mouth!

PSALM 40

To the chief Musician, A Psalm of
David.
I waited patiently for the
Lord, and he inclined unto me, and heard my cry.
He brought me up also out of
A horrible pit, out of the mucky
Clay, and set my feet upon a rock,
And established my goings.
And he hath put a new song in
My mouth, even praise unto our
God: many shall see it, and fear,
And shall trust in the Lord.
Blessed is that man that
Maketh the Lord his trust, and
Respecteth not the proud, nor such
As turn aside from lies.

To use your intuition to subconsciously perceive the meaning of this for you, look at and listen to the first word that comes to your mind. Now say that word out loud. Ask, "What is the exercise teaching me? How do I incorporate wisdom into my judgments?" Muse.

Hamlet, contemplating death, wondered if it would bring oblivion.

> To die; to sleep; to sleep? Perchance to dream!

Aye, there's the Rub; for in that sleep of death what dreams may come, when we have shuffl'd off this mortal coil, Must give us pause. (64-68)

> But that the dread of something after death,
> The undiscover'd country from whose bourn
> No traveller returns, puzzles the will . . .
> (78-80)

The reason for this fear of death, if that is what it is, is made more explicit in the three memorable lines of Shakespeare's presented above.

The book of Psalms has always inspired me. One day while I was reading the Psalms, the phrase from Psalms 39 and 40 jumped out at me. "While I was musing the fire burned." It became clear to me that I was a muser and was going to listen to my musings. The context meditation of David is an illustration of contemplation and seeking insights.

This portion of the psalms is now an inner mantra—Psalm 39: 2-7 and Psalm 40: 1-4. As you muse, notice what this song says to you!

As I was musing the fire burned. Then I Spake (spoke) . . .

Fire is a flame; passion is to be on fire to have faith to see fire, be passionate or enthused (one meaning from the Greek, Euthousia, is to be possessed by a god) a flame that is an intense feeling of passion.

My mystical self is one who sees the light. Seeing the light is to bring a desire into being. I saw the light and came to deep understanding of God and myself, a spiritual revelation.

Another result is that things became brighter, and I had more enlightenment and wisdom. I was no longer in the dark. In my study of mysticism, I found help in The Sufi Book of Life_that I quoted earlier. Refer back to it and read it again.

What I can learn from experience is who came to my mind. I recalled Goethe saying, "What thou hast is inherited from thy fathers; acquire to make it thine."

Tap into the creative wisdom of the past. What can the ancients teach me? The Ten Commandments are from old. The ethics of the Sermon on the Mount are vital and have a wealth of wisdom. Read them and must. Contemplate their wisdom.

Goethe also said, "and if this prime phenomenon makes him wonder, let him be content; nothing higher can it give him . . ."

Wow! It makes me wonder how much we have to give! Muse about the beauty of the universe and how that beauty is within, leading us to a knowledge of what we can do with life now.

The Psalm said, "He hath put a new song in my mouth." Be wise and live each moment in wisdom and with courage.

I don't like being in the dark about what is going on around me. I have experienced people who are dark souls; people who are bereft of understanding of what they are doing to cause themselves and others to have pain. They ooze anger and hurt. They do not see the light.

Jesus proclaimed in John 8:12 and 9:5, "I am the light of the world." The gospel of John opens with "in the beginning was the word." In the Greek, it is the logos.

The Logos who was life and the light of man.

I John 1:5—"God is light."

Geneses 1:2—God said, "Let there be light!"

As Disciple Mathew said in 5:14, "You are the light for all the world." So turn on the light of spiritual wisdom!

The man's soul was breathing murderous threats against the disciples when suddenly a light flashed from the sky! Saul became Paul, the Apostle. Paul saw the light.

Here is a set of instructions by one of my guides, Quaker and writer Thomas R. Kelly, for you to begin a practice of tuning into inward worship by turning to God for continuous practice. I have studied his book *A Testament of Devotion* on many occasions. A brief summary is below.

"Begin now, … in quiet, glad surrender to Him who is within…turn in humble wonder to the Light, faint though it may be…keep up the life of simple prayer and inward worship throughout the day. Let inward prayer be your last act before you fall asleep and the first act when you awake.

"…it takes constant vigilance and effort…because our lapses are so frequent and the intervals when we forget Him so long. It is rewarding because we have begun to live.

"…when you catch yourself again, lose no time in self-recriminations, but breathe a silent prayer for forgiveness and begin again, just where you are.

"At first the practice of inward prayer is a process of alternation of attention between outer things and the Inner Light. Preoccupation with either brings the loss of the other...Long practice indeed is needed...The plateaus in the learning curve are so long that many falter and give up, assenting to alternation as the best that they can do.

"The first signs of simultaneity are given when at the moment of recovery from a period of forgetting there is a certain sense that we have not completely forgotten Him. It is as though we are only coming back into a state of vividness that had endured in dim and tenuous form throughout."

We all sit at the feet of the Master who does all things well! There is no progress for us until we mindfully follow a prescribed exercise on a continuous plan. You will find that the mystic within is ready to reveal itself!

True spirituality will manifest itself in silence and quiet. Paul, the enlightened one, said to the saints in Ephesians, "Now, as Christians you are light." (New English Bible).

Ephesians 5:13, "But everything, once the light has shown up, is illuminated; and everything, thus illuminated, is all light."

Ecclesiastes 11:7 "Truly the light is sweet."

Both in Chicago and Arcata, I was a member of a group of ministers who met weekly to study Thomas R. Kelly's book, *A Testament of Devotion*. I encourage all of you to read this classic book on the light within us all as we practice God's presence.

In a state of reverie, our subconscious opens to us intuitively and symbolically, a path of life bringing about equilibrium and insight. Using your power of visual imagination, open your inner door to reveal new life, expanded love, and closeness to the Divine.

I follow a symbolic progression in this simple diagram for you to experience every word to its fullest.

Light

Logos

Love

Life

Luminous

Light will be incorporated in your life. Be joyful.

—Unknown

Rumi tells us the following in the book, *The Sufi Book of Life:*

O Hidden One, you fill East to West
Behind both moon's reflection and sun's radiance.
You are the water, and we are the millstone.

You are the wind, and we are the dust.
You are the spring, and we are the garden.
You are the breath, and we are the hands and feet.
You are the joy, and we are the laughter.

Perhaps life is calling you right now to withdraw from outer action on a project or relationship and to work behind the scenes. Steps taken in the inner world can have large effects. Or, perhaps you are being called upon to preserve some living wisdom or transmission until the time is ripe for it to be given openly again. Bide your time and reset it to the time of the One Being.

Now, it's in your hands! All of your inner voices can integrate into one. I urge you to stay the course. As you do, allow your inner self to continue to grow.

Collected Quotations—Read, cut out, enjoy! Then take the next step.

As soon as you trust
Yourself you will
Know how to love.
—Goethe

Seek the sacred within the ordinary.
Seek the remarkable within the commonplace.
-Rebbe Nachman of Breslov

God is voluptuous and delicious. . .

I
Have told you this time and time again:
If a person were in a rapture as great
As St. Paul once experienced and
Learned that her neighbor were in need
Of a cup of soup, it would be best to
Withdraw from the rapture and give
The person the soup she needs.
—Meister Eckhart

Only familiarity with
The thoughts of death
Creates true inner freedom.
—Albert Schweitzer

I was worried
About so many things
Like walking through cobwebs,
Then sloughing them off
One at a time.
—Anonymous

Here's the inevitable bad news about life. There are five
things we cannot change.

(1)   Everything changes. It's inevitable.

(2)   Things don't go as we plan.

(3)   Life is not fair.

(4)   There is going to be pain.

(5)   People won't always be loving or loyal.

But here is the good news. We can find happiness by embracing change. If we learn to accept those five facts instead of ignoring them, we will find ourselves blessedly liberated from their power over us.

Work can never tire you!
What tires you are
Your worries about the
Past and anxieties about
The future.
—Swami Parthasarathy *On the Cause of Stress*

To study the Way...
Is to study the Self.
To study the Self...
Is to forget the Self.
To forget the Self...
Is to be enlightened
By all things.
—Zen Master Dogen (1200-1253 AD)

Our doubts are traitors,
And make us lose the good we often might win,
By fearing to attempt.
—William Shakespeare, *Measure for Measure*

This marriage be wine and honey dissolving in milk.
This marriage be the leaves and fruit of a date on end.
This marriage be we laughing together for days on end.
This marriage, a sign for us to study.
This marriage, beauty.
This marriage, a moon in a light-blue sky.
This marriage, this silence fully mixed with spirit.

—Rumi

Here is a Parable:

Two South Sea Islanders were having a debate over ownership of a tree on the border of their properties.

A Trial was decided upon. The one who could stay the longest underwater would win.

Using rocks for ballast, they jumped in. When both failed to surface, divers went down and found both men dead, still clutching their rocks.

The cure of the part should not be attempted without treatment of the whole. No attempt should be made to cure the body without the soul, and if the head and body are to be healthy, you must begin by curing the mind."

—Plato

Live in the sunshine, swim the sea, and drink the wild air.

—Ralph Waldo Emerson

Here is one of my own mantras.
Let us reflect on wellness—Breathe!

Time is too slow for those who wait, too swift for those who fear, too long for those who grieve, too short for those who rejoice, but for those who love, time is eternity.

—Henry Van Dyke

Sometimes your joy is the source of your smile, but sometimes your smile can be the source of your joy.

—Thich Nhat Hanh

The wilderness and the idea of wilderness is one of the permanent homes of the human spirit.

—Joseph Wood Krutch

Learn from yesterday, live for today, hope for tomorrow.

—Albert Einstein

Rest is not idleness, and to lie sometimes on the grass under the trees on a summer's day, listening to the murmur of water, or watching the clouds float across the sky, is by no means a waste of time.

—John Lubbock

Be always at war with your vices, at peace with your neighbors, and let each new year find you a better man.

—Benjamin Franklin

Those of you who are scattered, simplify your worrying lives. There is one righteousness—Water the fruit trees, and don't water the thorns.

—Rumi

When the power of love overcomes the love of power, the world will know peace.

—Jimi Hendrix

How beautifully leaves grow old. How full of light and color are their last days.

—John Burroughs

When you possess light within, you see it externally.

—Anais Nin

We must begin thinking like a river if we are to leave a legacy of beauty and life for future generations.

—David Brower

Hope is like peace. It is not a gift from God. It is a gift only we can give each one to another.

—Elie Wiesel

A certain amount of opposition is of great help to a man. Kites rise against, not with the wind. —John Neal

Hope is itself a species of happiness, and perhaps the chief happiness that this world affords. —Samuel Johnson

In the depths of winter, I finally learned that within me there lay an invincible summer.

—Albert Camus

In every outthrust headland, in every curving beach, in every grain of sand is the story of the Earth. —Rachel Carson

The future is not something we enter. The future is something we create. —L. I. Sweet

"Because of the
Interconnectedness
Of all minds,
Affirming a positive
Vision may be about
The most sophisticated
Action any one of us
Can take."
—Willis Harman, 1918-1997

"Everything Flows."
—Heraclitus

There are two ways to be fooled. One
Is to believe what isn't true; the other
Is to refuse to believe what is true.
—Soren Kierkegaard

Each end
Of a spiral

Is the beginning
Of the next—
Designed for
Possibilities
A man's
True wealth
Is the
Good
He does in
The world
—Mohammed

With silence only as their
Benediction,
God's angels come.
Where, in the shadow of a great
Affliction,
The soul sits dumb.
—James Greenleaf Whittier,

Carl Sagan, the writer and astronomer, wrote the following to a friend on the death of his sister.

"Human misery is more often caused not so much by stupidity, as by ignorance, particularly our own ignorance about ourselves."

—Carl Sagan, author of *The Demon-Haunted World: Science as a Candle in the Dark.*

Prayer of Saint Francis of Assisi
Lord, make me an instrument of thy peace.
Where there is hatred, let me know love.
Where there is injury, pardon.
Where there is doubt, faith.
Where there is darkness, light.
Where there is sadness, joy.

O Divine Master, grant that I
May not so much seek to be consoled,
As to console;
To be understood, as to understand;
To be loved, as to love;
For it is in giving
That we receive;
It is in pardoning
That we are pardoned,
And it is in dying
That we are born to eternal life.
—Irish Poem, 10th Century

Avoiding death takes too much time
And too much care.
When at the very end of all,
Death catches each one unaware. —Peter Beresford

It really boils down to this—that all life is interrelated.
We are all caught in an inescapable network of
mutuality,

Tied into a single garment of destiny.
Whatever affects one directly, affects all indirectly.
—Martin Luther King, Jr.

The Trumpet of Conscience (1967)

I believe we are free, within limits,
And yet there is an unseen hand,
A guiding Angel,
Somehow like a submerged propeller,
Drives us on.
—Rabindranath Tagore

Success

To laugh often and much;
To win the respect of the intelligent people
And affection of children;
To earn the appreciation of honest critics;
To endure the betrayal of false friends;
To appreciate beauty;
To find the best in others;
To leave the world a bit better,
Whether by a healthy child,
A garden patch,
Or a redeemed social condition;
To know even one life has breathed easier
Because you have lived.
This is to have succeeded.
—Ralph Waldo Emerson

Happiness is a function of accepting what is.
Love is a function of communication.
Health is a function of participation.
Self-Expression is a function of responsibility.
Imagination is the eye of the Soul.

—Joseph Joubert

But when you have to turn into a chrysalis, you will some day you know,

And then after that into a butterfly, I should think you'll feel it a little queer, won't you?

Not a bit," said the Caterpillar.

—Lewis Carroll, <u>Alice in Wonderland</u>

Someday, after we have
Mastered the winds,
The waves, the tides
And gravity,
We shall harness for God
The energies of love.
Then for the second time
In the history
Of the world, man will have
Discovered fire.
—Teilhard de Chardin

Don't ask yourself what the world needs. Ask yourself what makes you come alive and then go do that. Because what the world needs is people who have come alive.

—Howard Thurman (1899-1981) Author, theologian, educator, and civil rights leader.

Death is not the greatest loss in Life.
The greatest loss is what died within us while we lived.
—Norman Cousins

Every time we go forward,
We leave something of
Ourselves behind.
—Shakespeare, *Hamlet*, Act II, Scene I

Hamlet— To be, or not to be: that is the question:
Whether tis nobler in the mind to suffer
The slings and arrows of outrageous fortune,
Or to take arms against a sea of troubles,
And by opposing, end them? To die...to sleep
No more; and by a sleep to say we end
The heartache and the thousand natural Shocks
That flesh is heir to. Tis a consummation
Devoutly to be wish'd. To die, to sleep;
To sleep, perchance to dream. Ay, there's the Rub.
For in that sleep of death, what dreams may come.
—Shakespeare, *Hamlet*

O death where is thy sting?
O grave where is thy victory?
Thanks be to God who gives us victory through our Lord
Jesus Christ.

—Bible: I Corinthians 15:55-7

I am condemned to freedom. I am not free because I can
make choices, but because I must make them, all the time,
even when I think I have no choice to make. I am free
because neither science nor religion can ever tell me, with
certainty, what my future will be and what I should do
about it. I am free to choose—whatever.

— Jean Paul Sartre

You must understand the
Whole of life, not
Just one little part of it.
That is why you must read,
That is why you must
Look at the sky,
That is why you must sing,
And dance, and write
Poems, and suffer, and
Understand, for all that is life.
—J. Krishnamurti

A Prayer for True Wisdom

Open my mind to that which is hidden from others.
Toward yourself have enough humbleness

To admit your mistakes, yet enough
Kindness to forgive yourself and others
Of their mistakes.
Looked for, it cannot be seen.
Listened for, it cannot be heard.
Reached for, it cannot be held.
Return to the sources of stillness.
That is the Way.

—Tao Te Ching

You cannot step in the same stream twice. And the wonderful secret is, you don't have to. —Heracutus

My summary judgment: Look ahead, plan ahead, be active, and don't let your disappointments become someone else's problem.

Andre Gide, the late philosopher-author, taught that as soon as one door closes another one opens. But too often we look at the closed door and disregard the open one.

I have explained this rather simply, but I think that you will get the gist of what I am trying to say. Juan Luis Borges' short biographical parable about Shakespeare, *Everything and Nothing*, says it so much better than I can.

"We are all characters in a play not of our writing."

To put it simply, things change—everything flows.

> **Within you there is a**
> **Stillness and a**
> **Sanctuary to which**
> **You can retreat at**
> **Any time and be yourself.**
> **—Siddhartha to Kamala**

I am circling around God, around the ancient Tower. And I have been circling around God for a thousand years, and I still don't know if I am a falcon or a storm or a great song.

—Rainer Maria Rilke

My belief of the interrelatedness of life can be summarized here.

> **My rhythm...Your rhythm...**
> **Me with you...Me alone...**
> **Together and apart. Each moving...**
> **Together...Apart...A part of...**
> **Apart from...Partners.**
> **Moving one...The other.**
> **Each aware...I of you...You of me.**
> **If you are willing to embrace it...Anything is possible!**

Like a Mirror

Like attracts like. The way we hope others will respond to us is the manner in which we must express ourselves.

Perhaps you have heard it said that a child's behavior reflects the manner in which he or she is treated. If he is treated with love, he becomes loving; if he is treated spitefully and is ridiculed, he becomes cruel and spiteful. To some extent the same is true in our lives. We get from others what we give, and we give to others what we have gotten. This is a basic function of our personalities.

Life is a mirror that reflects your expressions. If you smile, it reflects a cheery disposition. If you are irritable, it shows a true picture of your contemptible self. In essence, what you say of others is said of you. You will find nothing in the world that you will not find in yourself first. Nature takes on your moods. If you trust, you are trusted. If you love, you are loved. If you hate, you are hated. You will cast your own reflection.

Dear God, I am powerless and my life is unmanageable without Your love and guidance. I come to You today because I believe that You can restore and renew me to meet my needs today. Since I cannot manage my life or affairs, I have decided to give them to You. I put my life, my will, my thoughts, my desires, and my ambitions in Your hands.

I give You all of me: The good and the bad, the character defects and the shortcomings, my selfishness, my resentments and my problems. I know that You will work them out in accordance with Your plan. Such as I am, take and use me in Your service. Guide and direct my ways and show me what to do for You.

I cannot control or change my friends or loved ones, so I release them into Your care for Your loving hands to do with as You will. Just keep me loving and free from judging them. If they need changing, God, You'll have to do it; I can't. Just make me willing and ready to be of service to You, to have my shortcomings removed, and to do my best.

Help me to see how I have harmed others and make me willing to make amends to them all. Keep me ever mindful of thoughts and actions that harm others and myself, and which separate me from Your light, love, and spirit. And when I commit these errors, make me aware of them and help me to admit each one promptly.

I am seeking to know You better, to love You more. I am seeking the knowledge of Your will for me and the power to carry it out."

—Anonymous

Mind—As a Mirror

I have a body, but I am not my body. I can see and feel my body, and what can be seen and felt is not the true Seer. My body may be tired or excited, sick or healthy, heavy or light, but that has nothing to do with my inward I. I have a body, but I am not my body.

I have desires, but I am not my desire. I can know my desires and what can be known is not the true Knower. Desires come and go, floating through my awareness, but they do not affect my inward I. I have desires but I am not my desire.

I have emotions, but I am not my emotion. I can feel and sense my emotions, and what can be felt and sensed is not the true Feeler. Emotions pass through me, but they do not affect my inward I. I have emotion but I am not my emotion.

I have thoughts, but I am not my thought. I can know and intuit my thoughts, and what can be known is not the true Knower. Thoughts come to me and thoughts leave me, but they do not affect my inward I. I have thoughts but I am not my thoughts.

Golden Rules for Coping With Panic

1. Remember that although your feelings and symptoms are very frightening, they are not dangerous or harmful.
2. Understand that what you are experiencing is just an exaggeration of your normal bodily reactions to stress.
3. Do not fight your feelings or try to wish them away. The more you are willing to face them, the less intense they will become.
4. Do not add to your panic by thinking about what might happen. If you find yourself asking, "What if?" Tell yourself, "So what!"

5. Stay in the present. Notice what is really happening to you as opposed to what you think may happen.

6. Label your fear level from zero to ten and watch it go up and down. Notice that it does not stay at a very high level for more than a few seconds.

7. When you find yourself thinking about the fear, change your "what if" thinking. Focus on and carry out simple and manageable tasks and your power level will rise.

8. Notice that when you stop adding frightening thoughts to your fear, the fear begins to fade.

9. When the fear comes, accept and then except it. Wait and give it time to pass without running away from it. Recognize it and know it does not have to overwhelm you.

10. Be proud of yourself for your progress thus far, and think about how good you will feel when you succeed this time.
   —from B. Levine

From ***Your Body Believes Every Word You Say***, by Barbara Hoberman Levine—

"I firmly believe that life always works out for my benefit and my highest good. I sometimes will still question whether I am using my time wisely, but I now know that even so-called wasted time counts, especially if I don't judge myself so harshly and instead choose to enjoy each moment. Also, worrying about time or anything else will not ensure a better future and might actually make things worse for a while.

"There may still be buttons in me to be pressed, raw spots that need healing, but I will deal creatively with them. To be a healthy human being means that one will always have lessons to learn, challenges to face, problems to deal with, new opportunities for growth, and unconscious shadows to be brought into the light.

"Life may well be a journey with death the final destination, but it is meant to be lived as best as we can, as long as we can, no matter what. Living life, getting to know oneself, uncovering core beliefs, uprooting negative seed thoughts and planting healthy new ones is truly a life-long, never-ending process.

"…it is nearly 30 years since my left vocal cord was first paralyzed. With joy, I share the second edition of *Your Body Believes Every Word You Say*. Having written it, I understand more about myself, others, psychology, spirituality and health. I also have more faith in my ability and God's willingness to provide for me.

"Though from time to time I forget, I know that I am both the observer and the observed, the thoughts and the actions, the words and the deeds, the Creator and the Created. I am the process of my life. This knowing led to my healing, my mission in life, and this book, my bequest to the world." — Barbara Hoberman Levine

Maturity is the ability to—
    Do a job whether you're supervised or not.
      To finish a job once it is started.
        To carry money without spending it.
        And last but not least
The ability to bear an injustice without wanting to get
even. —Anonymous

And your body is the harp of your soul, and it's yours to
bring forth sweet music from it or confused sounds. . .
                    —Khalil Gibran

To come in contact with one who is realized,
Whose awareness is one with the stars,
The ocean, and people of all walks of life;
In the very presence of such expanded
    Awareness,
In the presence of such unconditional love,
You get a glimpse, a fire catches,
The worries get burned down,
The mind becomes so free.

If you learn how to listen, everything else will follow.
Everything flows.

Old wisdom in a new form. From the creative genius of
Goethe comes this message.

"There is one elementary truth, the ignorance of which
kills countless ideas and splendid plans. The moment one

211

definitely commits oneself, then Providence moves, too. All sorts of things occur to help one that never otherwise would have occurred. Whatever you can do or dream you can do, begin it. Boldness has genius, power and magic in it. Begin it now."

—Johann Wolfgang von Goethe

Happiness is a how, not a what; a talent, not an object.

—Hermann Hesse

Be glad of life
Because it gives you the chance
To love and to work
And to play
And to look up
At the stars.
—Henry Van Dyke

As soon as you trust yourself, you will know how to live.

—Johann Wolfgang Von Goethe

I believe that all bad things come to an end.

When you're feeling overwhelmed,
Step back and focus
On your higher power.
You'll find peace,
You'll gain a new perspective,
And you'll have the strength you need
To carry on.

Take time for yourself.
Curl up comfy cozy.
Have a good hard laugh.
Give in to extra helpings
Of tender loving care.
See the beauty of you.
Treat yourself as you graciously treat others.
—Anonymous

Imagination is far more important than knowledge.

—Albert Einstein

Do not take life too seriously. You will never get out of it alive.

—Elbert Hubbard

No man is an island entire of itself,
Every man is a piece of the continent,
A part of the main.
If a clod be washed away by the Sea,
Europe is the less,
As well as if a manor of thy friend's or
Of thine own were.
Any man's death diminishes me
Because I am involved in mankind.
—John Donne, Meditation on Man's Isolation

Perchance he for whom this bell tolls, may be so ill, as that he knows not it tolls for him; and perchance I may think myself so much better than I am, as that they who

are about me...may have caused it to toll for me...and therefore never send to know for whom the bell tolls; it tolls for thee.
—John Donne, Meditation on Mortality

Goethe said this well when he wrote—

Once the realization is accepted that even between the closest human beings infinite distances continue to exist, a wonderful living side by side can grow up, if they succeed in loving the distance between them which makes it possible for each to see the other whole against the sky. A good marriage is that in which each appoint the other guardian of his solitude.

On Friends

One of the best things about life is friendship. You find friends wherever you go. Friends are essential because they help bring out the best in you. When they see the worst, they still care. They just accept.

Friends are the stars in your happy memories. In your sad memories, they are the shoulders you leaned on and the hearts that listened. They just care.

Friends help you in your times of need. When things are going smoothly, they are content to be your friend. They just know.

Friends help create all your fun times, always there to spread laughter and joy. When you need tears, friends provide these, too. They just understand.

You, my friend, are all of these. And most of all, when you need it, remember friends just love, as I do you.

—Maria Elena Najera

That was one of the most fundamental and sacred duties good friends and family performed for one another—they tended the flame of memory, so no one's death meant an immediate vanishing from the world. In some sense the deceased would live on after their passing, at least as long as those who loved them lived. Such memories were an essential weapon against the chaos of life and death, a way to ensure some continuity from generation to generation, an endorsement of order and of meaning. To be nobody but yourself in a world which is doing its best, night and day, to make you everybody else, means to fight the hardest battle which any human being can fight; and never stop fighting.

—E.E. Cummings

The Eskimo shaman Igjugarjuk spoke to the Danish explorer Rasmussen.

"All true wisdom is only found far from men, out in the great solitude; and it can be acquired only through suffering. Privations and sufferings are the only things

215

that can open a man's mind to that which is hidden from others."

Sometimes we meet a person along life's way
And walk together,
If only for a little while,
And it makes all the difference.
Love consists in this—
That two solitudes
Protect and touch
And greet each other
—Rilke

Obstacles

We who lived in the concentration camps can remember the men who walked through the huts comforting others, giving away their last piece of bread. They may have been few in number, but they offer sufficient proof that everything can be taken from a man but one thing—the last of his freedoms. The freedom to choose one's attitude in any given set of circumstances, to choose one's own way.

—Viktor E. Frankl, *Man's Search for Meaning*

"The most beautiful thing we can experience," said Einstein "is the mysterious."

Here is the potential payoff from working with your dreams.

The single most important thing to understand about dreaming is that all dreams come in the service of health and wholeness. Every dream is a completely natural and spontaneous instinctive expression, welling up from your unconscious depths, directed toward bringing conscious awareness to neglected or represented aspects of your experience. The greater awareness of these inadequately appreciated elements of your life that come from paying more attention to your dreams always turns out to foster psychological and emotional growth and increasing maturity, creative expression, and developing awareness of your life's fullest potentials.

People will tell you that the secret to a good marriage is to be good pals, but most people don't treat each other like that. Become good friends with those you love.

Be able to recognize the new elements in a situation and to carve out new channels of thought and action appropriate to the new circumstances and calculated to achieve the desired results.

Unless one set his face in the right direction and make the start, he will not reach it.

Make these words a part of your beliefs. I keep a copy on my desk and read over them often, as I have spoken them often to you in this book.

Are you in earnest? Seize this very minute: What you can do, or dream you can, begin it; Boldness has genius, power, and magic in it. Only engage and then mind grows heated; Begin and then the work will be completed. — Goethe

Why do you want more knowledge when you pay no heed to what you know already?

But the fruit of the Spirit is love, joy, peace, patience, kindness, goodness, faithfulness, gentleness, and self-control; against such there is no law. And those who belong to Christ Jesus have crucified the flesh with its passion and desires.

If we live by the Sprit, Let us also walk by the Spirit.

—Galatians: 22-5

Francis of Assisi's Prayer for Healers

Lord,
make me an instrument of your health;
where there is sickness, let me bring cure;
where there is injury, aid;
where there is sadness, comfort;
where there is despair, hope;
where there is death, acceptance and peace.

Grant that I may not so much seek to be justified,
as to console;
to be obeyed, as to understand;

to be honored, as to love.
For it is in giving ourselves that we heal;
it is in listening that we comfort;
and in dying that we are born to eternal life.

The Prayer of St. Francis, as modified by Charles C. Wise.
This prayer appears in the beginning of Elisabeth Kubler-
Ross's *Death: The Final Stage of Growth* (New York:
Simon & Schuster, 1986)

Be careful of your thoughts
For your thoughts become your words.
Be careful of your words
For your words become your actions.
Be careful of your actions
For your actions become your habits.
Be careful of your habits
For your habits become your character.
Be careful of your character
For your character becomes your destiny.

What do you plan to
Do with your one wild
And precious life?
—Mary Oliver

Do not stand at my grave and weep.
I am not there. I do not sleep.
I am a thousand winds that blow.
I am the diamond glint on the snow.

I am the sunlight on ripened grain.
I am the gentle autumn rain.
When you awaken in the morning's hush,
I am the swift uplifting rush
Of quiet birds in circled flights.
I am the soft star that shines at night.
Do not stand at my grave and cry.
I am not there. I did not die.

There isn't always time to
Say goodbye. Therefore, we
Should always be sure we've
Given those familiar hands
One last squeeze.
—Friends of a girl killed in a crash

The moving words of Horatio, who knew Hamlet best, provide the best epitaph—

"Now cracks a noble heart. Good-night, sweet prince, and flights of angels sing thee to thy rest."
—William Shakespeare, *Hamlet*

God grant me serenity to accept things I
Cannot change; courage to change the
Things I can; and wisdom to know the
Difference.
—The Serenity Prayer

MUSE!

CONCLUSION

A friend's father was dying. He was an elderly minister and had founded a church. I said my good-byes and stepped back. The senior pastor offered a prayer. Then his daughter, sitting by his bed, took his hands.

Suddenly, he opened his eyes wide and looked up across the room. He said, "I will be with you my dear wife in just a little while."

We could tell he was fading fast. His daughter squeezed his hand and said, "Don't go!" He gently turned to her and said, "Let go, my dear!" She let his hand go and he took one long breath. As he exhaled, he closed his eyes.

His face had the most beautiful smile I had ever seen! The doctor came in and looked at him and said, "He is at peace and is happy!"

His daughter said, "He has gone to join my mom!"

Although tears were flowing, there was no sobbing. We joined hands. I mused in silent prayer. I said good-bye to a saint. "I hope I can die like that!"

END

BIBLIOGRAPHY

Alamas, A. H. *The Void* and *The Diamond Approach*. Shambhala Press, 2000.

Assagioli, Roberto. *Psychosynthesis*. New York: Viking Press, 1974.

The Act of Will. Turnstone Press, Northamptonshire, 1985.

Carson, Clayborne. *Autobiography of Martin Luther King, Jr.* Warner Books, New York, 1998.

De Chardin, Teilhard. *The Phenomenon of Man*, Harper & Row, New York, 1947.

Cousins, Norman. *Anatomy of an Illness*. Norton, New York, 1979.

Cummings, E. E. *Love and Life Poems*. W. W. Norton, 1962.

Donne, John. *Devotions Upon Emergent Occasions*. Ed. By E. T. Kruth, 1998.

Einstein, Albert. *Brainy Quotes*. Google, 2011.

Fox, Emmett. *Sermon on the Mount*. Golden Key Books, 2000.

Frank, Victor. *Man's Search for Meaning*. Beacon Press, 1992.

Gibran, Khalil. *The Prophet*, Albert A. Knoff, 1973.

Goethe, Johann Wolfgang von, Goethe's *Couplets and Dramas*. (1749-1832)

Higgins, William. *The Haiku Handbook*. Kodansha International, 1985.

Holmes, William. *Science of the Mind*. J. P. Tarchier, Penguin Press. New York, 2010.

Jones, E. Stanley. *Growing Spiritually*. Abingdon-Cokesbury Press, New York, 1953.

Kelley, Thomas. *A Testament of Devotion*. Harper Collins, 1966.

Kostenbaum, Peter. *The New Image of Personality*. Greenwood Press, Westport, Connecticut, 1978.

Letters to a Young Poet, BN Publishers, 2009.

Levine, P. *The Body Knows Every Word You Say*. Neil Winded, 2010.

Lilly, John C. *The Center of the Cyclone* and *Beliefs*.

Unlimited, Bantam Books, 1972.

Maslow, Abraham. *Toward a Psychology of Being*. Viking Press, New York.

Menninger, Karl. *The Vital Balance*. Viking Press, New York.

The New English Bible, Oxford University Press, 1970.

Parker, William. *Prayer Can Change Your Life* and *Guilty Grace*. Prentice-Hall, Inc. New Jersey, 1968.

Paul, the Apostle. *The Holy Bible. The Book of Psalms*.

Petrillo, Michael P. *Doctoral Thesis: A Study of Holistic Theory*. 1981.

Rogers, Carl. *On Becoming a Person*. Houghton Miffin, Boston, Mass. 1961.

Kubler-Ross, Elisabeth, *On Death and Dying*. Simon and Schuster, 1997.

Restock, Richard M. *The Brain*. Bantam Books, 2010.

Rilke, Rainer Marie. *Buddha in Glory*. 2003.

Turner, Audrey. *C. D. Blues*. 2011.

Tournier, Paul. *The Meaning of Persons*. John Knox Press, Richmond, VA, 1963.